Dedication

This book is primarily dedicated to my dear wife Linda, whose unfailing support through the thick and thin of life, since we met in 1973, has been above and beyond the call of wifely duty. With some complex issues, I have shamelessly used her nursing expertise by persuading her to sift and sort through nursing documentation in order to identify the key material which could support or augment the primary medical evidence. She has borne with fortitude the major domestic upheavals from some cases- the following are worth a mention:

The arrival of 118Kg of documents in 8 large boxes took over the house for weeks before the key material was identified and the report written

Over one weekend I was in charge of the original records (Two large suitcases worth) of some 50 living individuals whilst they were sorted and photocopied. Had any of them been taken ill over that period I was the primary reference point for any doctor who needed background information. The Judge ordered that they could not leave my side. Fortunately the process was accomplished quickly when the large Manchester firm of solicitors opened their office specially and brought in a team of secretaries to use four industrial sized photocopying machines. In two days all the records were copied, paginated into a master copy and then a further 12 copies made

The outcome of one high value civilian case rested heavily on my evidence. Unfortunately the case was scheduled for 10.30 am in Manchester on the Tuesday when we were due to arrive at Heathrow airport from Cape Town at 6.30 am. It was just do-able but only by using either a chartered helicopter or private limo (at their client's expense). This was potentially highly disruptive-not only did I have to lug my "Court Suit" on holiday in readiness and face a few hours giving evidence after a poor night's sleep but also Linda had to anticipate a few hours of abandonment in Manchester with all our luggage until I was released. As it worked out, I was informed by fax on the Monday morning that the case had settled and my presence was unnecessary.

Linda, thank you for your forbearance.

Dr Geoffrey Phillips FRCP

The Geriatrician in Court

Austin Macauley
Publishers Ltd.

A CIP catalogue record for this title is available from the British Library.

ISBN 9781786293107 (Paperback)
ISBN 9781786293114 (Hardback)
ISBN 9781786293121 (E-Book)

www.austinmacauley.com

First Published (2017)
Austin Macauley Publishers Ltd.
25 Canada Square
Canary Wharf
London
E14 5LQ

Acknowledgments

I would like to acknowledge the support and encouragement which I have received from consultant colleagues, junior doctors and numerous members of the nursing profession, both senior and junior. Special thanks are owed to my secretary/PA, Mrs Patricia Hunt, for her efficiencies, suggestions, speed and accuracy in typing up and finalising my medico-legal reports. Pat has done this over many years, as well as assisting in creating and typing this book.

Thanks are also due for the unfailing respect, courtesy and assistance which I have received from instructing solicitors, barristers, senior police officers, the CPS, judges and the many expert witnesses with whom I have had dealings. Even those barristers who "roughed me up" in court invariably sought me out after my evidence had been given in order to shake my hand.

Further thanks are due to the solicitors who provided actual material or pointers to the legal background for many of the cases illustrated. I freely acknowledge my gratitude for the vast amount of highly relevant legal case material available both in Wikipedia specifically and on the internet in general. I thank you all.

Prologue

This book is the sequel to Gnomic Wisdom but is of a completely different genre. It is of a serious nature intended to provide geriatricians and other physicians with guidance on medico-legal issues. It is a handbook/medical textbook of "how to do it" based upon some thirty years of experience in preparing medico-legal reports, attending court to give expert evidence and giving postgraduate lectures. With case illustrations it covers both medicine and aspects of the law (relevant to doctors), for the main areas where solicitors, coroners and police seek expert opinion from geriatricians. The book is structured as follows:

Chapter 1 Introduction, life expectancy, fitness decline, burdens of proof, criminal v. civil, prisons, tips on appearing in court, negligence, Bolam & Bolitho tests, falls, bed rails, fractured hips and subdural haematoma

Chapter 2 Pressure sores, senile squalor and Section 47 of the National Assistance Act of 1948

Chapter 3 Dementia, care facilities, mental capacity, testamentary capacity, contentious probate, "The Golden Rule", *Banks v. Goodfellow, Parker v. Felgate*

Chapter 4 Financial abuse and fraud

Chapter 5 Alleged and actual assault, bruising, sexual assault, emotional abuse, violence in dementia, fitness to plead/fitness to stand trial

Chapter 6 Swallowing problems, tube feeding, novus actus intervenius, causation of death, medication errors, resuscitation and use of care of the dying pathways

Chapter 7 Gross negligence, manslaughter by doctors, Adamako

Chapter 8 Diabetes, insulin, hypoglycaemia, murder and incompetence

Chapter 9 C. difficile, sloppy treatment, exhumation, GMC & fitness to practise

Chapter 10 Part 35 rules in the civil courts, preparing joint reports, getting started in medico-legal practice and arranging the "necessaries"

Chapter One

Medico-Legal Work

Opportunity, in the medico-legal field, knocked on my door early in my consultant career. A local solicitor, a fellow TA officer, was pursuing a case of negligence on behalf of his client – a man of 80 years, who had tripped over a very uneven pavement and fractured his wrist. The orthopaedic report identified the fall as causative of the simple fracture, which only needed treating with a plaster cast. The council had a clear duty of care to maintain the pavement. They could not deny breach of that duty and consequent liability for the uneven area of pavement, which they had neglected to repair, despite it having been drawn to their attention months before. The man was entitled to compensation and this was not disputed. It was the amount (quantum) which was at issue. The council noted that there was no loss of earnings involved and offered £X, based upon 8-10 weeks of decreasing pain, suffering and loss of amenity (function). It was assumed that full healing of the fracture would have occurred by then, with no adverse long term sequelae. I was asked to prepare a condition/prognosis report from my perspective as a geriatrician. I identified that, as is typical with the elderly, this man had been disproportionately affected. He had developed a fear of future falls and consequently had become reluctant to go out, which had progressed to him becoming housebound. The knock-on effects were social isolation and depression. I estimated that in addition, his care needs had been advanced by 2 years. On the balance of probability, I gave the opinion that in the absence of the fracture, his care needs would not have reached their current level naturally, due to the vicissitudes of ageing for 2 years. The judge preferred my evidence over that of the council's expert and awarded compensation of ten times the amount originally offered. Further cases followed and slowly but surely, referrals increased from further afield, as I became an established expert. Criminal work, initially mostly for the police, followed as my reputation grew.

Ideally, expert medical witnesses should be consultants of at least 8-10 years' standing, who are in active current practice. In certain specialties, especially those of a technical nature, such as surgery and cardiology where things change quickly, experts can rapidly become outdated after retirement. Geriatric medicine is not so technical and after NHS retirement in 2011, I opted to continue this aspect of my practice, until receipt of new instructions naturally "petered off" as time elapsed. I had expected that my currency as an expert would devalue with time. After 4 years, this had not happened and contrary to all expectation, my workload was increasing to levels involving some 150+ new instructions per year, of a mostly complex nature. Although I knew from judicial feedback, formal appraisal/feedback from SOCA (the Serious Organised Crime Agency who broker police expert work nationally) and repeated instruction from major firms of solicitors (both claimant and defence), joint instruction and requests from the GMC to screen complaints, I was still well respected in my field, I elected to decline new instructions from July 2015, whilst in my prime, rather than go on and on and risk going "off the boil". (One's reputation in the medico-legal field is constantly being informally and formally appraised with every new report by the relatively small world of experts, lawyers, coroners and judges – they do pass comment to each other without you knowing!)

Geriatric medicine is a boom area in the medico-legal field and there is a shortage of credible experts. The primary reasons are:-

- The fear of the unknown, especially appearing in court, discouraging new expert

- The difficulties in balancing the needs of the case with the restrictions imposed during the day by the 2003 contract (I never signed up to this)

- Current experts are now often retired from NHS practice and are winding down

- Referrals require a track record of medico-legal experience – no experience, no referral

There are some basic requirements over and above being an expert in your field. Experts need to be able to write a report to a very high standard and give an unbiased opinion to assist the courts. They need to be highly articulate in giving oral evidence and be able to think quickly on their feet when cross-examined. It helps considerably if they can impress the court by looking the part in dress and demeanour and by speaking confidently. They also need to be highly organised in being able to meet deadlines and to juggle various court attendances, often across the UK. With sometimes a very early start, many courts can be reached using the train by 10am. At any point in time, Experts can be asked to give their non-availability, for up to 12 months! They need to hold dates vacant until either a case settles or a court date is firmed up. They are essentially servants of the court and whilst every courtesy will be potentially offered to a busy consultant, the bottom line is that they can be ordered to appear as and when. Turning up late or not at all is totally unacceptable and at best will result in a judicial admonishment and/or a GMC referral. In extreme cases, they may have to bear the costs of a disrupted trial or be sentenced for contempt of court. Therefore taking on this work is not for the faint hearted or disorganised. It is however highly lucrative. The main downside is that payments are rarely prompt and sometimes solicitors insist on paying out at the end of a case – which can be 2 years later. Meanwhile, experts may have had to pay the tax on what was billed before receipt of any cash! It used to help to run the business as a company until the summer budget of 2015 removed the advantages.

Broadly speaking, case referrals are either of a civilian nature, requested by either the claimant's or defendant's solicitors, or of a criminal nature, either from the police or defendant's solicitors. Independent reviews for the GMC, Trusts trying to resolve complaints without recourse to lawyers and case screenings are sometimes also requested. Reports need to be structured around liability/breach of duty, causation and current condition/prognosis. My regular repertoire of core medical issues included bruising; CDT; delirium; dementia; dehydration; falls/fractures; pressure sores; testamentary capacity and life expectancy. I found it useful to have standard generic discussions for these key areas, which I could incorporate into reports, to assist the courts in understanding how I had arrived at my specific case-by-case opinions. Some negligence issues result from bad luck, minor mistakes/errors of judgement, but in other cases the sheer degree of stupidity and ignorance can be truly shocking. Wilful idiocy of a reckless nature can result in criminal charges of gross negligence/ manslaughter. Because of the very complex and specialised issues involved, the decision to charge doctors with criminal negligence can only be made by two highly specialised CPS units (based in York and London).

The epidemic of mesothelioma, due to historic occupational asbestos contact before effective legislation reduced exposure, is just now reaching a peak as the time lag between exposure and disease can be 40 years. The main issue of causation is normally dealt with by chest physicians. However, geriatricians are becoming increasingly involved, preparing reports on the peripheral issues which can represent most of the compensation "absent the mesothelioma, how long would Mr X have lived and how long would he have remained fit enough to have provided care for his disabled/demented wife/widow and avoided her current care costs? Take into account and opine on Mrs X's likely trajectory of decline and her life expectancy and indicate when her needs would have exceeded his caring abilities." This is four-dimensional chess! These complex claims are normally for the order of over £500,000. Because of their high value they are dealt with in the High Court and very able lawyers on both sides are usually involved. Opinions in these areas and on these cases need to be handled along logical lines.

Life expectancy – The estimation of the future life expectancy of an individual is a very inexact science, regardless of the methodology employed. Actuarial tables, by the law of large numbers, allow an average life expectancy to be projected. This is the starting point. The methodology used widely by the insurance industry to determine individual risk is set out in "Medical Selection of life Risk" by R D C Brackenridge, R S Croxson and Ross McKenzie (5th Edition, 2006). However, the life expectancy of an individual is determined by a complex mix of genetic and environmental factors and chance. Perusal of records will reveal lifestyle factors, diseases or risk factors which will indicate whether life expectancy is likely to be greater or less than the average for the relevant age group cohort. Because of the high prevalence of smoking in the past, many of the risks for smoking in the elderly are already factored into the tables and may not warrant significant further discount.

Fitness – As a general rule of thumb, most elderly persons can expect that only the last third of their projected future life expectancy will be accompanied by significant disability, with only the last few months associated with profound ill health. Light caring activities of a supervisory nature and ordinary spousal duties can usually be performed up until those last few months of profound ill health. It is only the ability to perform the heavier domestic chores and the heavier caring spousal duties (involving lifting or which are regularly accompanied by disturbed sleep) that declines in a linear manner during the last third of an elderly person's projected future life-expectancy.

Criminal cases have to be proven to the high standard of "beyond reasonable doubt" which is 99%

certainty. Most of the hassle involves the criminal work and it often pays relatively poorly at legal aid rates. The trials can drag on and experts can be kept hanging around for days at the whim of the court – whilst the cases can be very interesting they are best declined at the outset by busy NHS consultants. Parole board assessments sometimes provide the opportunity to visit prisons to assess a prisoner's fitness and likely risk to the public if released. Beware of these cases – one very elderly diabetic prisoner who had spent much of his adult life in prison for sex offences was considered to be at low risk of repetition and released on licence. He obtained a private prescription for Viagra from a GP unaware of his background and resumed his offending. He spent the rest of his days behind bars. Prison categories are:

- CATEGORY A – For prisoners deemed to be of risk to the public and/or with the desire and support/means (possibly external) to escape

- CATEGORY B – For prisoners at high escape risk but lacking the means and support to so do

- CATEGORY C – For prisoners not at high escape risk but who could be opportunists

- CATEGORY D – For prisoners of no risk to the public and of no escape risk

Visiting a prisoner needs to be planned well in advance and permission of the governor obtained – get the solicitor to do this. All prisons have very tight security checks on visitors – including doctors. Try to carry as little as possible – stethoscope, pen and paper is all you need – other bits of medical equipment will be available in the prison medical centre. Anything deemed contraband or unnecessary will not be allowed in. Do you leave valuable stuff (mobile, money, house keys, and handbag) in the car? I always considered car parks for prison visitors (which are never very close to the prison gates) to be potentially dangerous places to park. They tend to be frequented by the criminal fraternity who can be opportunists! Female doctors are advised to look and dress as plainly as possible.

Civilian cases have to be proven to the lesser standard of "balance of probability" which is more than 51% certainty. These cases rarely actually get to court as most are settled by agreement/compromise to avoid the loser bearing the costs of the trial. The conduct of these cases is governed by very strict part 35 rules which apply both to lawyers and experts. They dictate tight time-frames for all and cases can be thrown out if one side is deemed to be "timed-out". Experts must give unbiased evidence for the court, not evidence biased to one side. Almost all these civilian cases stand or fall on the quality of the expert evidence. Clever and creative lawyering moves can seriously wrong-foot experts. The classic trick is for the claimant's solicitor to disclose all the evidence (as they must) but in a large bundle (2-3000 sheets) of disorganised and often irrelevant records in the hope that the single page of evidence damaging to a claimant's case will be missed by the defendant's expert. It is not unheard of for them to photocopy everything else twice, shuffle it and randomly insert that one page. If the expert misses it, it's the expert's fault. Experts need to know what ought to be there and look for it. If it's not there then comment upon the absence! There are, however, lots of other clever legal moves along the way which can hassle experts by leaving the deadlines short.

- The need for a meeting (on the phone normally) with the other side's expert to set out areas of agreement and disagreement in a joint report – normally the claimant's expert is the scribe.

- Answering questions posed by both sides.

- Having to hold dates vacant in case of a trial. Each side will try to gain the upper hand through their expert being more available than the opposition.

Coroner work normally comes on the back of an initial report for the police which has found insufficient grounds for criminal charges. Sometimes coroners commission their own reports when the case is controversial. Coroners run their own fiefdoms and standards vary. Technically an inquest is held to establish the cause of death by answering the questions- who, what, how, when and where (but not the why) if the death may not, at first sight, be due to natural causes. An inquest conclusion is based upon "balance of probability" and ought not to apportion blame in a way which could be used by other courts in a negligence claim. However there is provision for the coroner to add neglect as a rider under the "Jamieson rules". This applies where there has been a gross failure to provide basic medical attention to a person in a dependent position which has directly caused or materially contributed to their death. Examples may include the failure to put in place a pressure relieving care plan when indicated or the failure to switch on a non-invasive ventilation aid for someone with COPD. Some coroners will determine cause of death without recourse to an inquest. Others will give a family with grievances their time in court. This inevitably results in the interested parties being "lawyered up" including typically – the family, the Hospital Trust, the GP and the Community Trust if there has been DN input. Thus 4 solicitors, each accompanied by a barrister, will be present and eager to ask questions. These inquests can drag on as the issues expand if the coroner fails to get a grip. Inquests involving industrial accidents, health and safety issues and deaths in custody must have a jury but the coroner can summon a jury in any cases. Those elderly persons subject to a deprivation of liberty order (DoLs) who die need to be referred to the coroner.

Most doctors at some point in their career will be subject to a GMC complaint. These are often malicious, unfounded complaints which lead nowhere. They are screened out by expert opinion early in the process. The bottom line is that they go nowhere if the doctor's standard has merely fallen below but not seriously below standard as a one-off. Any attempt at the cover-up of an honest mistake or error of judgment almost always results in standards being deemed to be "seriously below standard". In that event, trouble looms.

Appearing in court is an alien concept to most people and the run up to a trial can generate considerable anxiety. Doctors can appear in any of the three categories of witness, which are:

Witness to fact – they just happen to be doctors who have witnessed something happening which is unrelated to their job

Professional witness – describing what they saw and did in their professional role, often treating the injuries following an accident or assault.

Expert witnesses – normally have had no active professional role but are asked to give an opinion after the event – they are the only witnesses who can give opinion under oath, everyone else is limited to outlining what they saw and did.

Facts are for courts, not experts, to determine. It is not uncommon for experts to have to give alternative opinions depending upon which facts the courts determine to be true.

A typical criminal case involving a medical expert will have been investigated by the police and that evidence will be reviewed by the expert whose opinion will be crucial when submitted to the CPS for a decision as to whether to prosecute. The expert's contact details will be passed to "witness care" who will update them on the pre-trial progress and give due warning of the trial date. They will be your principle contact, though the CPS solicitors may have met with you to check out your degree of certainty about your opinion –they will want no surprises in court. The CPS will then appoint a barrister to prosecute. The role of the prosecution is to build an unassailable wall of evidence. The role of the defence is to breach it thereby causing the jury to have reasonable doubt. They may have their own expert whose opinion is likely to contradict yours. Experts ought to have seen each other's reports and commented thereon before the trial. Perfect planning prevents pathetic performance. On the day of the trial there are some "tips" which if followed prevent problems:-

- Double check your report for any stupid errors or inconsistencies and re-evaluate whether you are still of the same opinion. Take a copy with you

- Decide early what you will be wearing. A suit is expected but it ought to be comfortable, tidy and preferably not brand new. It ought to be the sort of suit that the judge and barristers wear, not the sort that a defendant might have bought from the supermarket two days earlier

- Decide how you will be travelling (avoid driving on the day – hold-ups will wrong foot you badly) and whether on the same day or the night before and organise train tickets early to avoid queuing. Early morning trains are generally very reliable. There is a fairly high chance that on these early trains one of your fellow passengers will be a barrister, judge or witness who could be involved in your trial – so keep your own counsel. If travelling the day before, witness care will sort out accommodation but remember that other guests may also have involvement in your trial

- Make sure that you have had a good breakfast – lunch breaks are rarely before 1pm and not all courts have canteens

- Always arrive at court earlier than you were told. There is "airport security" to pass through. Then report to an usher. If you are a "Crown witness" witness care will be alerted and look after you. There will be normally be a room exclusively for prosecution witnesses with tea, coffee, water and toilets – use the former sparingly and the latter frequently. You ought to be kept informed as to progress and when you are likely to be called. As a Crown witness you cannot discuss the case with other witnesses or hear any evidence until after yours is given. If you are a defence witness the usher might alert the defence team to your arrival but you will basically be left to your own devices and have to sit in the public areas with the criminal fraternity who will not be hard to identify. (The really scruffy ones carrying a hold-all, wearing a face like a robber's dog are expecting to be sent directly to jail upon sentencing). You are best checking the court listing and lurking near the allocated courtroom in the hope that you can catch the eye of one of the defence team. Defence witnesses can sit in court throughout and will usually be sat behind defence counsel and expected to advise them on awkward questions to pose to prosecution experts

• Check whether the judge is "your honour" or "your lordship" in case you need to address them directly. Long wigs and the more red and frills in the robes are good indicators of seniority

• Make the usher aware as to whether you wish to swear an oath or affirm. When your time comes use this to test the acoustics of the courtroom

• Give your evidence standing, not sitting. Not only does this look more professional but it keeps you more alert. Position yourself comfortably so as to face the judge and jury – they are the only important ones in court. Turn head and shoulders to receive questions from barristers but turn back to the comfy position to deliver answers facing the judge and jury

• If you are a "Crown witness" you will be called early in the trial to give your evidence "in chief" to assist prosecuting counsel in building their wall of evidence. You will be controlled very tightly as you are taken carefully through your report – yes or no answers will probably be all that they want. Stick to that unless told otherwise. Giving evidence in chief could well take an hour or so.

• Immediately afterwards, and normally without a break, you will be subject to cross-examination by the defence counsel. This could be another couple of hours. They will aim to discredit your evidence and opinion.

• Beware of the over pleasant approach. That normally means that they are confident about leading you to a position which suits their client. If the questions become aggressive you are probably doing a better job than was expected

- Be on your guard for some classic ploys

- The prefatory statement will be phrased, "I am sure that you are aware of the important work of Prof. Jones in this area. Could you then please tell me why your opinion…" Now you are potentially in trouble! You have either heard of Prof. Jones and his work or not. If you have never heard of him and he is truly important your credibility in the eyes of the jury will falter if you admit your ignorance. There will be strong temptation to "blank" the bit about Prof. Jones. If you do you have effectively agreed that he is important – leaving the way open for his ideas, however eccentric, to be introduced and undermine your evidence. It is better to admit ignorance of his work on the basis that if he was that important in your field of expertise you would have heard of him and his work. If you are right counsel will move on. If you are wrong and he is the world authority you're stuffed, especially if he is the one sitting in court advising the defence team.

- A good defence counsel can slowly inch by inch move you into a position where they can suddenly demand an inappropriately simple yes or no answer to a very complex issue. If you failed to see it coming all you can do is appeal to the judge for a ruling on the basis that there is a danger that you could mislead the court by giving too simple an answer to complex issues

- After cross-examination and hopefully after a break for lunch, prosecution counsel will again have their turn to quiz you to reverse any perceived damage to their case

• Normally after giving your evidence you will have the opportunity to hear the expert evidence put forward by the defence.

Civilian cases of negligence normally start with proving liability to provide a duty of care. For bodies such as the NHS, nursing homes, and councils the duty of care cannot normally be denied. The next step is proving that there was a breach of that duty of care according to the "Bolam standard" – where clinical negligence is claimed, the Bolam test is the one used to determine the standard of care owed by professionals to those whom they serve, e.g. the standards of care provided to patients by doctors. The case *Bolam v. Friern Hospital Management Committee* (1957) established that if a doctor acts in accordance with a responsible body of medical opinion, he or she will not be negligent. The Bolam principle is clear that the standard of care must be judged by the standards of a practitioner of the same specialty and the same grade. This is because practitioners from differing specialties and grades will have different knowledge and experience and this leads to differences in approach, in potential awareness of risk, and a different differential diagnosis for any clinical situation.

Many have heard of the Bolam test without knowing the full background. The full details as described by Wikipedia were:-

Mr Bolam was a voluntary patient at mental health institution run by the Friern Hospital Management Committee. He agreed to undergo electro-convulsive therapy. He was not given any muscle relaxant, and his body was not restrained during the procedure. He flailed about violently before the procedure was stopped, and he suffered some serious injuries, including fractures of the acetabula (hip). He sued the committee for compensation. He argued they were negligent for:

1) Not issuing relaxants

2) Not restraining him

3) Not warning him about the risks involved

McNair J at the first instance noted that expert witnesses had confirmed that much medical opinion was opposed to the use of relaxant drugs, and that manual restraints could sometimes increase the risk of fracture. Moreover, it was the common practice of the profession not to warn patients of the risk of treatment (when it is small) unless they are asked. He held that what was common practice in a particular profession was highly relevant to the standard of care required. A person falls below the appropriate standard, and is negligent, if he fails to do what a reasonable person would in the circumstances. But when a person professes to have professional skills, as doctors do, the standard of care must be higher.

In this case, the verdict was in favour of the defendant hospital. Given the general medical opinions about what was acceptable electro-shock practice, they had not been negligent in the way they carried out the treatment.

Subsequently, this standard of care test was amended – the Bolitho amendment – to include the requirement that the doctor should also have behaved in a way that 'withstands logical analyses regardless of the body of medical opinion. The determination of whether a professional's actions or omissions withstand logical analysis is the responsibility of the court.'

Having established duty of care and breach of duty, the next step is to identify the consequences – what that breach of duty caused. The final step is quantifying the adverse consequences. General pain, suffering and loss of amenity will be worthy of compensation by way of general damages. There may be special damages worthy of a claim for specific areas of detriment.

It is estimated that every year more than 1 million patients and care home residents suffer avoidable harm. Some 5.6% of patients suffer from serious and avoidable bedsores. Falls are the next most frequent cause of avoidable harm. The classic trip hazards at home are cats, mats and dressing gowns. The latter are often old, warm, well-loved and long-reaching to just above the ankle. Gradual loss of height from osteoporosis results in dressing gowns reaching the floor and causing falls.

In hospitals and care homes the frail but mobile elderly mostly fall near beds or in bathrooms whilst transferring position and the actual fall is rarely witnessed. Falls from beds are common. Serious injuries can result which can be lethal or life-changing.

Fracture to the hip in the older person is a devastating life event, associated with significant mortality and morbidity. Up to a third of those sustaining such fractures die within 12 months. Of those who survive with normal cognitive function, only 50% gain independence but often to a level of function below that which they enjoyed before the fracture. In the presence of dementia the majority of the survivors are left with such a degree of disability, that independent living is impossible, and they enter residential or nursing homes. Surgical repair is standard treatment as these fractures rarely heal without intervention and normally prove fatal if untreated. The primary purpose of surgical repair is to stabilise the fracture and in so doing reduce the pain which would otherwise persist from the broken bone edges grating upon one another on movement. Without stabilisation the provision of basic nursing care is almost impossible without pain. Pressure sores and pneumonia result from inactivity. The need for strong painkillers will aggravate immobility and predispose to pneumonia. The secondary (but still very important) purpose of surgical repair is to allow rehabilitation to commence very soon after the fracture and before there is significant muscle wasting in the legs from disuse.

Even minor head injuries can have serious consequences. Subdural haematomas are collections of blood clot in the subdural space within the skull but outside the brain. This space contains bridging veins and a slow venous bleed may result spontaneously or more usually from head injury if the veins rupture. Brain atrophy (shrinkage) which accompanies great age puts these veins under tension increasing the risk of rupture. The resistance of the vein walls to tears also deteriorates with age. As a result subdural haematomas are common in the elderly and typically present some days or even weeks (depending on a number of factors including the rate of bleed/ooze) after a trivial and often unremembered head injury. The venous ooze may cease early and result in only a small collection which can be easily accommodated around an atrophic brain. These can be asymptomatic. More usually the clot expands slowly eventually causing neurological signs as the brain is squeezed. Some smaller clots can stabilise and resolve with time and are managed conservatively. Others require burr hole drainage to remove the clot. Aspirin and warfarin increase both the risk and rate of bleeding and deterioration can be rapid.

Brisk bleeding from anticoagulation will only cease when the clot has expanded such as to raise the pressure within the skull sufficiently above venous pressure. Inevitably the brain will be severely squeezed. Rapid deterioration in levels of consciousness and large clots are bad prognostic signs and are normally a harbinger of death. Older individuals, even if not frail, lack the physiological reserve (stamina) to recover from neurosurgery and generally fare badly. There is a very high perioperative mortality rate. If they survive the immediate aftermath of neurosurgery there is often severe residual brain damage and older patients rarely return to anything approaching previous levels of function. Full time care in a nursing home is very often required. It is thus common for neurosurgeons to decline to operate in "the best interests of the patient" when the prognosis for meaningful recovery is very poor.

Falls – The upright human being is intrinsically unstable. Falls in the young and fit are rare, simply because good eyesight, efficient hearing and normal sensation in the limbs give early warning of environmental hazards, which are compensated for by supplety of the limbs, muscular strength and a brain, which is quick to act, to alter bodily position accordingly. By contrast, failing eyesight, deafness and decreased sensation in the limbs make the frailer older person less aware of their surroundings and reaction to normal hazards is impeded by decrease in muscular strength, arthritis and slow brain functioning – partly the result of the normal aging process, which is made even worse in the presence of dementia. Paradoxically, the slower walking gait, which comes with ageing, enhances the tendency to fall. Even in the best institutions, falls can never be entirely prevented without so restricting patient autonomy to a degree which would constitute abuse. However the preventative measures as recommended by NICE Guideline CG161 can reduce the likelihood of falls, especially in the absence of dementia or confusion. Those measures are less successful when there is confusion because such patients undertake risky manoeuvres and may not remember to summon assistance.

Cot sides – The use of restraints and cot sides/bed rails in institutions is controversial and opinions as to the wisdom of their use have varied over the years. There is no doubt that they prevent small accidental falls in unwell restless patients but on the other hand, confused and agitated individuals may see them as a challenge and in attempting to climb over them, risk more serious injury. The assessment of risk/benefit in the use of cot sides is very subjective and can and often does change day by day. Pressure alert mats can give warning of the imminent potential for a fall from bed but can only prevent falls if the staff are vigilant.

The other main causes of harm were urinary tract infections linked with catheter use, blood clots and poor monitoring of anticoagulants. Drug errors including giving the correct dose to the wrong patient, whilst common, rarely cause serious problems. Figures released by the NHS litigation Authority (NHSLA) on legal costs for the 4 year period ending in 2014 indicated the payment of some £502m to just ten top law firms including damages and costs. Whilst the government is trying to reduce the legal costs, claimant legal firms claim that their costs consistently amount to less than 10% of the compensation secured for claimants. They also indicate that the costs could be kept low if the NHSLA admitted liability earlier in the process in clear cut cases instead of defending them.

Chapter Two

Pressure Sores

There are an estimated 180,000 newly acquired pressure sores developing each year in the NHS. In 2011 there were over 90,000 pressure sore related patient safety incident reports, making pressure sore prevention one of the biggest patient safety challenges facing the NHS.

Evidence indicates that the majority are preventable and could be avoided through simple actions by staff, patients and carers. As well as causing long term pain and distress for patients, treatment is estimated to cost the NHS between £1.4 and £2.1 billion per year. There is a good strong evidence base on how to prevent pressure ulcers from developing. On over 200 occasions I have assisted both civil and criminal courts on matters concerning pressure sores and have lectured at national level twice on the subject.

Whether civil action for negligence will succeed will be determined by the following 3 tests:

i) Has the risk to an individual patient been adequately assessed?

ii) Have timely and appropriate preventative measures been put into place, commensurate with the risk?

iii) Has the situation thereafter been appropriately monitored and suitable action taken if the sores fail to improve or worsen?

Normally within a hospital or care home there is no wilful or reckless disregard of care but merely suboptimal care in some or all of the above which is enough to prove negligence to the civil standard. I illustrate this with the case of Mrs D R which, following my report was settled by the NHSLA for a substantial sum.

I was asked to provide a report upon liability, condition and prognosis dealing with the circumstances and consequences of this lady developing a pressure sore on her sacrum following admission to hospital on 07/10/11.

Mrs D R, then an independent 82-year-old lady, had recently returned from holiday in Spain and was admitted to hospital on the 07/10/11 with a severe community acquired pneumonia. This required immediate treatment in intensive care where she remained until transfer to ward 3B on 24/10/11. On transfer there were no pressure sores. By 04/11/11 she had developed pressure sores to the sacrum and later on the right foot. The sacral sore remained present in February 2013 though was slowly healing. It was alleged that inadequate preventative measures were taken causing the sores to occur. After detailed review of the extensive records, my opinions were:-

- In my opinion, by virtue of her severe pneumonia, age and underweight status, this lady was at significant risk of pressure sore development from the time of hospital admission. The fact that no sores developed whilst she was extremely ill in the intensive care unit suggests that her risk there was appreciated and appropriate preventative measures taken. The transfer documentation when she moved to ward 3B clearly recorded her high risk of pressure sore development.

- In my opinion, the preventative measures taken on ward 3B were suboptimal and negligent. There was lack of monitoring of the situation as evidenced by the gaps in the safety and comfort check sheets which started on 24/10/11 until 27/10/11 and a delay in providing a pressure relieving mattress until after there was evidence of sacral damage. There were further delays in providing a cushion to facilitate her sitting out for the purposes of allowing physiotherapy to commence and no formal repositioning regime was started until 11/11/11 by which time the sore had deteriorated. As evidenced by the tissue viability referral of 17/11/11 there was further deterioration. The tissue viability assessment of 18/11/11 suggests that regular repositioning may not have been optimal. The ward round concerns of 05/12/11 suggest medical dissatisfaction with the nursing care on ward 3B because there had been sore progression after 18/11/11. Ward transfer was arranged.
- Following transfer to ward 3C, matters stabilised and then began to slowly improve suggesting that with a proper preventative regime, sores would probably have been avoidable.
- It was my further opinion that the consequences of the sores developing from negligence on ward 3B were to cause pain, suffering and added detriment to her health and quality of life which was still persisting almost 12 months following eventual hospital discharge. As such it is likely the sores delayed her rehabilitation

and prolonged her hospital stay. Her current disabilities, which were permanent and likely to worsen due to the vicissitudes of age, were due to the pressure sores.

- The sacral sore impacted disproportionately upon her quality of life and depressed her mood by permanently restricting her ability to sit. It was uncertain whether this sacral sore will ever heal and if it heals, when it will heal. Even if the sore heals it should be considered to be only temporary healing. Further breakdown is very likely to occur because the healed area will be much more at risk of breakdown than skin which had never been damaged. As such her ability to sit will be permanently restricted in order to prevent recurrence. In addition she will permanently require the same maximal care measures and equipment simply to minimise that enhanced risk. It would be reckless to step-down those measures regardless of whether the sore ever heals. Those maximal measures included her pressure relieving bed, portable shower, adjustable chair and pressure relieving cushion and in-chair sling. My opinion was that absent the development of the sacral sore those maximal measures would not have been necessary. This case was settled for a substantial sum.

Pressure sores, in addition to prompting civil litigation, can lead to police investigation and criminal prosecution. They were previously known as bed-sores and now are usually called pressure ulcers by professionals. For court reports I continued to use the better known term of pressure sores. I shall make some general observations about pressure sores, based upon my personal experience and with reference to the relevant literature (NICE Clinical Guidelines 2005), available at www.nice.org.uk (GC029). There are further more recent updates. These observations of mine concern the development, classification, prevention and management of pressure sores, as follows:

Although historically, a number of different classification systems have been used, the European Pressure Ulcer Advisory Panel classification system of pressure ulcer grades is now standard and grades the sores into one of four categories, as follows:

1) Grade 1 – nonblanchable erythema of intact skin, which is the heralding lesion of skin ulceration
2) Grade 2 – partial thickness skin loss with superficial ulceration, blister or shallow crater
3) Grade 3 – full thickness skin loss with some damage below the skin. The ulcer presents clinically as a deep crater
4) Grade 4 – full thickness skin loss with extensive destruction and deep tissue necrosis, which may involve serious damage to muscle and indeed bone. Such deep pressure sores may progress to deep infection, leading to septicaemia (blood poisoning) and death

The superficial sores of grades 1 and 2, whilst common, are normally short-lived and if they heal quickly are rarely consequential. It is the deep grade 3 and 4 sores which are the real scourge. Their presence can and often does result in police investigation. Normally the scenario which leads to police attention is that someone frail is admitted to hospital from the community (either from their own home or care home) with one or more horrendous large deep gangrenous grade 4 sores. They often look dreadful and the stench can be appalling. Some can be the size of cannon balls. Nurses, especially the inexperienced, will often be shocked and launch an Adult Safeguarding Investigation by social services who, if they suspect neglect of a vulnerable adult, will involve the police. If death has occurred due to septicaemia directly from infection within the sore the coroner will be informed and will action police investigations. The police will collect the evidence available which will normally include some or all of the following:

- Photographs
- Medical records/care home records/district nursing records
- Post mortem results, usually from a PM conducted by a Home Office pathologist
- Statements from staff normally taken under caution
- Expert evidence and opinion as to whether there has been neglect

The expert opinion will be crucial in determining what criminal charges, if any, are made. Options range from gross negligence/manslaughter at the top end or if the victim lacks capacity due to dementia, charges of neglect of a vulnerable adult can be made using the mental capacity act. Expert advisory reports need to be very detailed and opinions mainstream, measured and reasoned by being set against the natural history and pathology bearing in mind that some sores are never preventable.

Frail elderly individuals are particularly susceptible to pressure sores due to various intrinsic factors. These may include immobility, incontinence, malnutrition even without loss of fat padding, anaemia, oedema, low albumin levels, along with cardiac disease and poor circulation, which may be aggravated further by dehydration.

Various risk calculators, such as the Norton, Braden and Waterlow systems, have been developed in order to provide a structure and consistency to patient assessment. They certainly raise awareness, provide a minimum standard of risk assessment and in so doing, provide a crude indicator of risk and thereby provide a framework for use of specialist equipment. They are, however, limited in certain aspects and the evidence on the accuracy of pressure ulcer risk scales is confusing and it is not clear that the scales are better than clinical judgement. {One problem which regularly arises is the under-scoring of risk, often due to inexperience and lack of training in using a particular tool. In this respect the Braden scoring system (where the lower the score the higher the risk) can be problematic. It is used much less than the Waterlow scoring system (where the higher the score the higher the risk). This has led to some very unfortunate assumptions of low risk by individuals inexperienced with the Braden system who have assumed that low scores equate to low risk}.

Sores of grades 1 and 2 and some of grade 3 start superficially and are visible on the skin surface from the outset. They normally follow a superficial break in the integrity of the skin and if they are neglected and become infected, they erode deeper and can become grade 4 sores. Skin maceration by moisture (e.g. incontinence and sweat) and skin shearing by rough handling or self-movement on a wet bed with creased sheets are the common causes of the initial skin break.

Deep pressure sores of grade 4 often do not start as superficial skin breaks. They start deep and the overlying skin may initially seem normal. Sometimes there is also coincidental superficial damage which then can erode in and meet deep tissue damage moving outwards.

Typically deep grade 4 sores result from direct unrelieved pressure over bony areas. The hips, heels, buttocks, shoulders and elbows are particularly susceptible in dependent patients. Tissue damage can occur when high pressure is exerted over an area of skin for a period as short as a few hours, or more commonly, when lower pressures are exerted over a prolonged period. This disrupts the microcirculation in a wedge of tissue that is overlying the bone. The widest area of deep and irrevocable damage is closest to the bone and invisible on the skin. The deep tissue damaged becomes necrotic (dies). It then moves outwards eventually revealing itself suddenly as a fully developed and often malodorous grade 4 sore. Such sores can appear on the skin surface from seemingly nowhere as quickly as overnight. The process would normally be painless to the individual. Before the sore reveals itself fully as a deep ulcer on the skin there will usually be some firmness palpable deep under the skin caused by the dead tissue working its way towards the skin surface. There may be some redness visible just prior to skin breakdown. These however are subtle signs and would normally only be picked up if specifically sought by a qualified nurse. Even if these signs were found and pressure relief given, it would make no difference to the outcome – dead tissue will come to the surface eventually.

The timing between deep tissue death and skin ulceration depends largely on the toughness of the tissues and the distance between the skin surface and the deep damage. Over the buttocks and in someone obese it may take up to 10 days for the deep damage from the pressure sore to reveal itself on the skin surface, and less than 5 days in someone less well nourished. The heels are normally much more dense and tough and even though the distance between skin and bone is less it still could take up to a week between damage and ulceration.

It is widely contended that 95% of all pressure sores are preventable by simply relieving pressure. This is usually done by repositioning the patient every 2-3 hours, ideally at a 30 degree tilt, and additionally supplying an appropriate pressure relieving mattress. The 5% of those which are not preventable include terminally ill patients on a very steep trajectory of decline. Reduced skin perfusion, resulting from the dying process as other organs fail, dramatically enhances the vulnerability to pressure sores in the weeks prior to death. The sacral area is particularly susceptible, resulting in the so-called Kennedy Terminal Ulcer. They also occur in those who have lain immobile on a hard surface for a long period, prior to being admitted to hospital, e.g., falling and breaking a hip or falling due to stroke.

Once pressure sores develop into open wounds, best practice requires the seeking of advice from a Tissue Viability Specialist Nurse. Specialist dressings including medical grade Manuka honey are available. If deep wounds require surgical débridement (excision of dead tissue either using a scalpel or using maggots) or if systemic infection requires treatment, hospital referral may become necessary. If they are left unattended they will become infected. If they are not dressed and heavily contaminated with moist faeces and urine, infection will progress to septicaemia and death rapidly over the course of 7-10 days, perhaps less in someone very debilitated. That deterioration is usually associated with a painless decline accompanied by drowsiness and reluctance to eat or drink. There may be no fever but there may be a delirium with confusion and consequent loss of mental capacity. Progress to death may appear peaceful. Untreated, death is certain. Even with hospitalisation and very active intervention, the prognosis is very poor and especially so in someone with co-morbidities.

Even with the best treatment, sores may not heal in the presence of co-morbidities. Their ongoing presence saps strength and vigour, rendering patients prone to further unrelated infections. Such further infections further sap strength and vigour, halting and reversing any healing that may have occurred and cause further deterioration. Sores can set in train a vicious circle of terminal decline.

The Senile Squalor Syndrome

The senile squalor syndrome, sometimes called Diogenes syndrome, is an unusual condition seen mostly, but not exclusively, in elderly people.

Over the age of 60, approximately 1 person per 2000 is affected per year. The condition is not a disease as such and is not a psychiatric illness, as these people show no evidence of psychiatric disease. It appears to be a positive reaction against the usual standards of personal and environmental hygiene and may represent the end stage of a lifelong personality disorder. The main features are as follows:

i) Gross self-neglect

ii) Social isolation

iii) Extreme squalor

iv) Indifference to their surroundings

v) Often an extremely offensive odour in and around the house

vi) Rubbish hoarding and reluctance to tidy or to throw anything out

In their younger days, they were usually of normal to high intelligence, previously socially competent and often held down responsible jobs. Often there was past evidence of an independent streak, with them becoming gradually more reclusive, stubborn and quarrelsome as the years progress. They mostly live alone, with a preponderance of females to males.

Section 47 of the 1948 National Assistance Act

This historically useful tool was on the statute book until 2014 but is due to be repealed. Unbelievably by the standards of today it sanctioned the compulsory removal of people of sound mind with full mental capacity from their homes. The details and background were:-

Section 47 of the original 1948 National Assistance Act gave the Medical Officer of Health the power to apply to a magistrate, for the compulsory removal of persons who were:

i) Suffering from grave chronic disease or being aged, infirm or physically incapacitated, or were living in insanitary conditions

ii) Unable to devote to themselves and were not receiving from other persons, proper care and attention

It required 7 days of notice, to authorise a person's detention in a suitable hospital or other place for a period not exceeding 3 months. During the 7 day period of notice matters could and in one widely publicised case, did deteriorate dramatically, which led to the Act being amended, as next.

National Assistance (Amendment) Act of 1951

This allowed compulsory removal to be immediate, provided that the opinion of the Medical Officer of Health was supported by that of another Registered Medical Practitioner. It was considered to be best practice for a geriatrician to be in that supporting role.

The period of detention was limited to 3 weeks. This Act was used about 250 times per annum in the UK until the turn of the millennium but its use diminished rapidly thereafter. The main problem was that compulsory removal was associated with a high mortality rate, and as such, even if done for overwhelming reasons, could not be said to be in the person's best interest.

The recent Law Commission's final report on adult social care law called for the repeal of section 47, because "it is hard to interpret, difficult to implement and seems to breach the European Convention on Human Rights". The Commission said other provisions, such as those in environmental health legislation, the Mental Health Act 1983, and the Mental Capacity Act 2005, provided a more appropriate means of caring for people in distress.

The death of EP (below) combined elements of the senile squalor syndrome and death from a neglected pressure sore.

The Death of E P

In 2011 I advised West Yorkshire Police on the death of E P whose daughter, A, was convicted of gross negligence manslaughter at Preston Crown Court in the summer of 2012. Although matters were fully reported in the press at the time I shall use initials rather than names. The details were:-

I was asked by them to provide a report on the circumstances, which surrounded the death of E P (DOB 1928), on or before the 10/05/11. Specifically, I was asked to give an opinion as to whether the actions of her daughter, A, amounted to gross negligence/ manslaughter. I was provided with details of the essential elements required to fulfil these charges and my remit was as follows:-

i) To comment on the condition of the home and how that would impact upon the health of E P and A
ii) To comment as to whether the home was in a suitable condition to meet E P's needs
iii) To comment from the photographs and accompanying information as to whether A neglected to care for E P and if so whether there was a causal link between this and her death
iv) Life expectancy of E P had she received adequate attention
v) Likely effects of her Parkinson's disease if left untreated
vi) Likely effect of the use of food grade Manuka honey as sole treatment for the pressure sores
vii) Likely effects of malnutrition upon E P's physical condition

The deceased, E P, was an 82-year-old lady who resided at home with her daughter, A, who worked part-time, two days a week. E P was housebound and had not been seen by neighbours for some years. She was last seen by any doctor, in a fracture follow-up clinic in 1998. She had previously fallen and fractured her right olecranon (elbow). Following fixation, she was discharged home to the care of her daughter, in late 1997, at which time she was described as mobile without aid and able to manage stairs. The photographs of the house in 2011, and the report of R T, speak for themselves in revealing appalling living conditions, typical of the senile squalor syndrome. The house had few utilities, no running water and was crammed full of rubbish. E P's bed was not recognisable as a bed. It was basically a pile of rubbish.

At around 23.00 hours on the 10/05/11, A took her mother to the A&E department by car, where she was found to be cold, rigid and devoid of signs of life. Death was declared at 23.20 hours and the police contacted. As illustrated by the post mortem photographs and described in detail by Dr W in his forensic post mortem report, she was cachectic and had multiple pressure sores.

I noted from the general practitioner records the following:

i) The lack of any recent records

ii) A hospital letter from July 1985 which describes her as "this strange lady"

iii) No evidence of diagnosed or treated Parkinson's disease or dementia

I noted from the summary of the witness statements the following:

i) M B, an electrician, who attended the house in July 2010 observed the extremely unkempt state of the house and accompanying rubbish

ii) C G, a friend of A, who had never visited her home. She had, however, accompanied A out recently (April 2011) on a day trip

The post mortem photographs record the situation as described by Dr W in his post mortem report. I highlight from them the following:

i) An appearance consistent with cachexia (emaciation)
ii) Grade 4 pressure sores over the left lower jaw, the upper chest and buttocks.
iii) Grade 2 pressure sores upon the left ear
iv) That her head was bent forward and to the left such that the pressure from the chin on the chest wall and the pressure from the left shoulder on the left ear could have accounted for the chest, lower jaw and ear sores
v) The post mortem report concluded that E P died from pressure sores, with Parkinson's disease and malnutrition being significant contributory factors (the Parkinson's disease was presumed on the sole basis of brain histology)

Photographs of the house spoke for themselves in revealing a gross degree of squalor, well beyond even extreme "normal" neglect and untidiness. They were typical of the senile squalor syndrome.

I made my usual observations on pressure sores in general and gave the opinion that once pressure sores develop they require careful assessment and treatment to limit their progression and prevent infection and death. At the very least they required the provision of a specialist pressure relieving mattress and/or cushion, together with a regular turning regime. This was not done. Specialist dressings for the wounds and pressure relieving equipment for use at home are easily accessed by the district nurses. Manuka honey, albeit food grade, was used by A upon E P's sores and I observed that this was just about acceptable as a dressing. However, honey produced as a food is often not well filtered, and may contain various particles. Medical grade honey processed for use in wound care is passed through fine filters, which remove most of the pollen and other impurities, to prevent allergies. Also, although honey does not allow vegetative bacteria to survive, unfiltered honey does contain viable spores, including clostridia. It is therefore not without risk of causing disease if applied to open wounds. The failure to seek a formal professional nursing assessment, (which would have resulted in the provision of pressure relieving aids, more modern dressings and on-going monitoring of the situation) was totally unacceptable, as new sores could develop and existing sores worsen.

In my opinion, the state of the house was typical of the senile squalor syndrome and consistent with this syndrome having been present for some years, possibly beginning shortly after the death of Mr P years earlier. To the 'lay' person, the state of the house would represent a health hazard to the occupants. In actual fact, disease to the occupants rarely results from the insanitary conditions, presumably because the slow accumulation of rubbish fosters, in the occupants, a natural resistance. It is therefore my opinion that the condition of the home alone, may, in fact have had little impact on the heath of either E P or A.

By virtue of her age, possible dementia and likely very poor mobility, E P was a progressively vulnerable adult, as she declined in health and especially once she developed pressure sores. She was in need of medical assessment, nursing supervision and medication. This she had not received for some years. Her escalating needs were neither being met by the state of the house, nor her daughter and there is no evidence that her general practitioner was aware of her deteriorating status. The likelihood is that it was E P herself who was originally responsible for refusing any offers of help and that at one time, she may have had sufficient capacity to exercise her right to decline medical help and live her life with a degree of autonomy. This can be very difficult for doctors and nurses to deal with effectively, even if they are aware of the full picture. They often are not, unless someone has drawn their attention to it. Once alerted, in my experience, the only way forward is to implement a Section 47 Order of the National Assistance Act of 1948 and compulsorily remove persons, such as E P, to a place of safety. The law requires certain conditions to be fulfilled. Those conditions were being progressively met over the months prior to her death. No professional is likely to have known that her condition had declined, simply because the only person who could have raised the alarm was A. This she did not do.

By virtue of E P's aged and infirm status, her daughter may have had a 'duty of care'. This was for the courts to determine – which they did. It seems unlikely that A was suffering from significant traits of the senile squalor syndrome. The supporting evidence from the statement of C G and the fact that A was still in employment, strongly suggests that it was E P not A who had the much more extreme trait of this syndrome, which compounded her vulnerability.

The pressure sore over the buttock appears to be a grade 4 and is consistent with a period of immobility, sitting semi-upright in either bed or in a chair, for at least 12 hours. This may have occurred some days, weeks or even months prior to hospital admission. Any incontinence would have aggravated matters. The position of E P's head is consistent with untreated Parkinson's disease and suggests that she had been in slow decline for months. This would account for the sores upon her chest and left ear.

Her general practitioner, who had a professional duty of care, could have acted if he/she had been contacted, even if E P had retained capacity and consistently refused to attend surgery or refuse entry to the house. A Section 47 Order could have been implemented when the situation deteriorated, if the full circumstances were known. In this respect, the only person in a position to know of E P's decline was A. It was she who failed to raise concerns when she could and should have done so.

Had Parkinson's disease, immobility, pressure sores, malnutrition and possible dementia been diagnosed and optimally treated, her quality of life would have been enhanced, with the likelihood that she would not have suffered unnecessarily and not have died in May 2011. Life tables would give an average future life expectancy of 9 years for an 82 year old female. Even if E P had advanced Parkinson's disease, immobility and dementia, her life expectancy with basic care, would have been more than 1 year beyond May 2011.

I summarised matters for the court as follows:-

- A appeared to have been a responsible adult, whilst E P was a very vulnerable adult, technically in her care.
- The courts had already determined that she had a legal duty of care.
- A must have noticed that E P was deteriorating and needed professional help. A was the only person who could have alerted the authorities to the deteriorating situation and in this she failed. Had she alerted the authorities, either by contacting the general practitioner, or by way of a 999 call earlier, the

probability is that E P would have either been taken to hospital, or received professional care at home, before the malnutrition and pressure sores had progressed with the further likelihood that she would not have unnecessarily suffered and that she would have survived.

• It was therefore my opinion that A's failures resulted in the premature death of E P. It was my further opinion that her failures to provide for E P's essential basic needs and her failure to summon assistance when her condition deteriorated, constituted gross negligence.

• As evidenced by the post mortem examination, E P was emaciated without evidence of causative underlying disease. In my opinion, and despite the assertions of A that E P had been eating adequately, there had been an obvious, serious and prolonged imbalance between her energy intake and energy expenditure. She had, in effect, been slowly starving.

• Over the months prior to May 2011 A progressively failed to meet E P's escalating physical needs in respect of nutrition and her pressure sores. The care she gave was progressively inadequate.

• The consequences of this slow starvation would, at the very least, have been progressive weakness from muscle wasting. The use of wasted muscles is usually painful leading to further reluctance to move. This would have enhanced her tendency to develop pressure sores and to impair the healing of those sores which had developed.

• She would have become too weak to eat and possibly to drink adequately. The further consequences of the starvation from lack of care would have been to progressively sap E P's strength and vigour, enhance her vulnerability, and set in train a vicious circle of decline.

• Matters would have been worsened by the onset of a low grade infection from the pressure sores and any anaemia or vitamin deficiencies from her poor diet. She is likely to have been disinterested and unlikely to have interacted with A in the positive way which A asserted.

- In my opinion it would have been progressively unlikely that E P would have retained her capacity, strength and force of character, to have resisted appropriate and urgently necessary professional interventions delivered in her best interests. Such professional assistance was denied to E P simply because A failed to set it in train as she ought to have done.

The Case of E B. This case was very similar but differed in that his son W B actively resisted help which was on offer for his father. The details were as follows:-

E B was a 92 year old man who lived alone, being loosely supervised by his son W B. Concerns about the health of E B had been repeatedly expressed for years. Specifically, E B had been wandering from his home, both by day and by night. Numerous attempts by social services to provide assistance had been actively resisted by W B. At some point during the summer of 2013 W B had apparently agreed with social services that he would live with his father. In August 2012, E B was assessed as lacking capacity to acknowledge his vulnerability to risk, from choosing to go out alone. It was very likely that there was a background of dementia and strong evidence of incontinence. As evidenced by his BMI of 18, he was underweight by December 2013. Matters came to a head at Xmas, when police were called to the house by ambulance staff, whose wish to admit him to hospital was being obstructed by W B. As a result of police persuasion, E B was taken to hospital and admitted.

In essence, he was frail and cachectic, confused and had pressure sores, the most serious of which were grade

4 sores to the right buttock area and to the right heel. His health declined, culminating in his death 14 days later. Following post mortem, the cause of death was given as:

1a Bronchopneumonia

1b Pressure sores and a deep buttock ischio-rectal abscess

2 Ischaemic heart disease

After reviewing the evidence my opinions were:

- E B was on a steepening trajectory of decline during the latter part of 2013, which seemingly steepened further from early December 2013, with the onset of reduced mobility and reluctance to eat. This, coupled with his tendency to sleep on chairs (some of which were covered with plastic sheets) and incontinence, would have greatly enhanced his risk of pressure sore development. He developed serious grade 4 sores, with the likelihood that a low grade infection set in, adding detriment to his condition and further accelerating his decline. With proper assessment and care at home, these sores would have been preventable. The most serious pressure sore was a grade 4 sore over the buttock, which was consistent with a period of immobility, sitting semi-upright in either bed or in a chair, for at least 12 hours. The deep damage most likely occurred some days or weeks prior to hospital admission and progressed thereafter to the state visible in the photographs. The deep damage probably occurred between mid-November 2013 and not after the first week of December.
- There was strong evidence to support the contention that E B lacked capacity and as such was extremely vulnerable. W B has acknowledged that he had a 'duty of care'. E B's initial care, perhaps until as

late as early November 2013, was conceivably consistent with good intentions on the part of W B, which were out-paced by E B's rapid decline, associated with reduced mobility, reluctance to eat, incontinence and reduced cooperation with the inexperienced care, which W B was attempting to give. Thereafter and over some weeks prior to Xmas 2013, W B progressively failed to meet E B's escalating physical needs, in respect of nutrition and general care. This would have progressively sapped E B's strength and vigour, enhanced his vulnerability, and set in train a vicious circle of decline. The inadequate care W B gave caused unnecessary suffering. It ought to have been obvious to W B that he was failing to meet E B's needs and that professional assistance was urgently required. Such professional assistance was not just denied to E B, simply because W B failed to set it in train, as he ought to have done. He had actually been instrumental in resisting help which had freely been on offer.

- In addition to the detrimental effects of the grade 4 sore over his buttock, there were clear other physical manifestations of E B's decline which should have been obvious to W B and indicated to him that E B needed formal professional attention. These were:

i) The onset of reduced mobility, reluctance to eat and noticeable weight loss.

ii) His persisting incontinence such that the chairs he chose to sleep upon had to be covered in plastic sheets.

iii) The additional pressure sores evident from the photographs which were present on the heel and the shin. These would in all probability have been more readily visible to W B than the buttock sore if he had been caring for E B properly.

My overall opinion is that W B's resistance to accept help and his failure to summon assistance, when E B's condition deteriorated, constituted wilful negligence, in the sense that he recklessly continued with inadequate care, to the detriment of E B. Why he did so, was for the courts to determine.

W B was charged with ill treatment or neglect of a person who lacks capacity, contrary to section 44 of the Mental Capacity Act 2005. He was advised by his legal team to enter a guilty plea. He refused. When alternative opinion gave the same advice he elected to defend himself. The jury found him guilty and he received an eighteen months custodial sentence.

The Case of M I

In the case of MI who was found dead at home on 01/11/12, I attended a disgusting scene of death to advise the police on the likely circumstances, which surrounded her death at the age of 83. She had died in a bed so sodden with liquid faeces and urine that there was a permanent hollow in the mattress. Faeces and urine lay in a copious trail between the bed and bathroom. By contrast the rest of the house was relatively clean and tidy. There were two sons. The police were investigating this as a gross neglect/manslaughter case but were uncertain as to whether such charges were justified. They also needed advice on the likely timings of her deterioration to help them decide whether one or both sons ought to be charged. Crucial to that decision was expert opinion as to whether the state in which she died would have been apparent on 29/09/12.

She lived with her son, Jimmy who provided care for her and was in receipt of the Attendance Allowance for so doing. Jimmy was described as reclusive, lacking social skills and not being highly educated. M I had a long history of extremely poor personal and domestic hygiene and had stubbornly refused offers of help repeatedly over the years. She had been incontinent for years. She avoided contact with health care professionals and social services, preferring to depend upon Jimmy. Over the years her mobility had declined progressively such that she had become confined upstairs in her bed for many months prior to her death. There was no evidence to suggest that she lacked the mental capacity to choose to continue her way of life. When her other son William visited her on 29/09/12 he thought that despite the efforts of Jimmy her situation was declining. He thought she was of sound mind and capable of coherent speech when she refused his offers of help, even to simply clean her up and provide clean clothes, he acquiesced and did not seek external help for her. Neither Jimmy nor William sought any help during the following weeks and William made no attempt to ask after her health. He was unaware of her decline after 29/09/12. She died 33 days after his visit.

The causes of death included sepsis and cardiorespiratory failure due to severe skin ulceration and infection, bronchopneumonia, acute myocardial infarction and terminal hypothermia. The conditions in which she had been lying were considered to have been the central factor in her death. I highlighted the following:

- That at death she was lying in bed on her right side in the foetal position with her legs crossed. There was evidence of extensive, gross faecal and urinary incontinence over her body, the bed and surrounding floor tracking to the landing.

• There were extensive pressure sores over the right hip and lower legs where they were crossed. These appeared to be deep grade 4 sores, with no dressings covering them. They were heavily contaminated with faeces. The right hip and buttock were lying in the deep "pit" in the mattress with evidence of a "tide-mark" across the buttocks suggesting that this area had been immersed in liquid at some recent time.

• The bed was very heavily contaminated by both urine and faeces. There were no features of the senile squalor syndrome in the dwelling and food and drink were present in the kitchen.

I applied the basic principles to formulate my opinion on the likely timeline for her terminal decline. In my opinion, the principle cause of death was septicaemia from the pressure sores. I would not have expected her to have survived untreated septicaemia for more than a maximum of 10 days and it could have been as short a period as 5-7 days from onset to death. Given the heavy faecal contamination I would have expected the septicaemia to have started within 24 hours of full skin thickness breakdown. I would have also expected that it would have taken between 5 and 7 days for the skin to have broken down fully to expose deep damage and precipitate the onset of the septicaemia. Each of these time-frames could have been much shorter given her frailty. Extrapolating the maximum figures backwards we have (10 + 1 + 7 = 18) and with the minimum figures we have (5 + 0 + 5 = 10). Basically her final terminal decline could have started 10-18 days prior to death, i.e. any time between 14/10/12 and 22/10/12. It is unlikely that she was anywhere close to the state in which she died when William saw her 33 days earlier.

It was my further opinion that, to the untutored eye of Jimmy, she could have appeared “normal” with retained mental capacity and stubborn resistance to accepting help until septicaemia took hold 5-10 days prior to death, clouded her consciousness and rendered her incapable of resisting help. At that time medical help ought to have been sought, though even with hospitalisation and very active treatment, the probability is that she still would have died. The state of the house overall was not at all typical of the senile squalor syndrome and was more consistent with Jimmy making inadequate attempts at cleanliness and being thwarted by the results of worsening incontinence upstairs. The state of the bed and immediate surroundings is consistent with a longstanding insanitary state which significantly worsened over the 2-3 weeks prior to death.

The evidence suggested, to me, that Jimmy, who had a duty of care, was fulfilling that duty, within the constraints of his mother’s wishes, until early October 2012. Thereafter, her trajectory of natural decline began to steepen and he began to struggle with coping with her needs without any support. Had help been requested during the first two weeks of October, and had she accepted that help then the outcome may have been different. The evidence further suggested that her trajectory of decline dramatically steepened during her last 2 weeks of life as she developed pressure sores and septicaemia. At some point she most likely lost her vigour and mental capacity to resist any help. By that time it is likely that Jimmy was completely out of his depth and unable to provide the necessary care for her. He could and should have requested help as he would not have known that, by that time and even with help, her chances of survival were very poor. Why he did not do so is unknown, he may have continued to respect his mother's long held views to refuse help, he may have not have realised how ill she had become, or he could have realised how ill she had become and wilfully chosen to do nothing about it.

The CPS declined to prosecute and no-one was charged.

CHAPTER THREE

Up to 25% of the elderly population have significant dementia with many of them being dependent and residing in formal care homes. Some 16% of people over the age of 85 years live in care homes. Most care home residents have significant dementia often coupled with physical illnesses. The average and median time spent in Nursing Care prior to death is between 2 and 2.5 years. For the slightly fitter individuals needing lower level Residential Care both the average and median time spent is slightly longer at between 2.5 and 3 years – the exceptional ones who live longer than this tend to be those whose functional abilities were prematurely stepped down and whose disability was advanced suddenly by a one-off traumatic event rather than by progressive on-going disease taking its toll on life expectancy. Those who die within weeks or months of placement tend to be those on a steepening trajectory of decline perhaps further steepened by the trauma of re-location.

Formal Care Facilities, Care Delivery, Problems

My experience of residential and nursing homes derives from having performed in excess of 8000 domiciliary visits during my career with increasing proportions of patients being seen in formal care facilities rather than in their own homes as the years progressed. In the 1980's and early 1990's most people were seen in their own homes, but following the rapid expansion of care home provision from the mid 1980's as NHS long stay units closed, the most needy requiring domiciliary assessment were in formal care facilities. Domiciliary visiting on an ad hoc basis (often on the day of request) by consultants from a wide range of specialties (even general surgery) was commonplace in the 1970's and early 1980's but was progressively discouraged in most specialties to save money (it attracted an additional fixed fee roughly equivalent to 1.5 hours of salary). Only psychiatrists and geriatricians continued to provide that service in significant numbers. Domiciliary visiting as an extra was effectively killed off by the 2003 consultant contract though some specialties dedicated fixed sessions to provide it though, at the cost of flexibility and rapidity. Putting matters into perspective, 5 consultant geriatricians serving a population of 400,000 in Liverpool during the late 1980's performed some 1500 domiciliary visits annually at the additional cost of roughly one WTE consultant. The numbers of them done progressively declined over the years and after I retired in 2011 the numbers dwindled to a handful.

Most care homes, in my experience, provide holistic care at a satisfactory standard. A handful are exceptionally good and some are very poor with the variance often due to the quality and staffing levels within the homes. Death rates, for obvious reasons, are higher than the average for the age group cohort. Sometimes deaths cluster or there is a constellation of untoward events which prompt an investigation into standards. These investigations can be of variable standard, often historically focussing on the paperwork rather than the actual care. When problems occur in NHS psycho-geriatric units (especially those isolated from main-stream hospitals), in-house investigations tend either to default to a "whitewash" or else go the other way and facilities are closed down and police investigations launched.

One psycho-geriatric unit was subject to the "white-heat" of a major police investigation over many months, which after reviewing hundreds of records and obtaining statements from many relatives (whose perceptions of care provision covered the full range of opinion from exceptionally good to exceptionally bad) identified some 17 cases where the medical care was considered to have possibly been suboptimal. I reviewed these cases with the following conclusion: "Having reviewed and briefly summarised the evidence on these 17 cases, I have identified some suboptimal areas of care. They were relatively trivial and inconsequential in four of the cases numbered. One of the cases received more seriously suboptimal care (having not been given the most appropriate antibiotic) most likely due to the inexperience of the doctors whose actions, though they were well intentioned and may have seemed reasonable as the events unfolded were, with the benefit of hindsight, below the standard of general hospital physicians. They were not however general hospital physicians. The Bolam principle in law is clear that the standard of care must be judged by a practitioner of the same specialty. As such their actions did not amount to neglect or ill-treatment. It is only probable but far from certain that his death was a consequence of the suboptimal care. As regards another case the contra-indications to anticoagulation (active peptic ulceration and subdural haematoma) were so obvious that his death would not have been preventable. The reasoning for not giving anticoagulants ought to have been recorded. The fact that it was not was technically negligent but as few experienced doctors would have used them it was inconsequential. I found no areas of concern in the other 11 cases reviewed." No police action resulted. However, the unit was closed down, psycho-geriatric care to a large community seriously disrupted and senior consultants decamped and secured alternative posts elsewhere.

In another psycho-geriatric unit a "whistle-blower" (nurse A) claimed that one of her nursing colleagues (nurse B) was causing the death of patients by claiming that they were in pain and as a result persuading the doctors to prescribe Fentanyl patches in increasing strength until death intervened. The unit was closed and staff, including some senior consultants, were suspended and a lengthy and very costly police investigation commenced. Remaining staff were redeployed and worked in a climate of suspicion and fear for over 12 months. Although use of Fentanyl was high for an average psycho-geriatric unit, I concluded that it was thoughtful and appropriate for the individuals receiving it who were genuinely in pain and reluctant to take oral medicines. There was no evidence of anything untoward and certainly nothing criminal. There was a historic culture within the unit to use Fentanyl borne from the experiences of one of the doctors who had some previous experience having worked in a pain clinic. Interrogation of the records revealed that, contrary to the assertion of nurse A, nurse B did not suggest Fentanyl prescription any more frequently than any of her colleagues. Many suspended staff left the profession or took early retirement. It later turned out that the "whistle-blower" nurse A was a renowned "fantasist" who was forever making up stories. Although staff knew this they declined to mention it to the detectives in case attention was drawn to themselves. She had a long psychiatric history and had been "sectioned" in her student days.

I have also advised Police on 5 separate occasions where "whistle-blowers" made allegations of murder in various care homes throughout the UK, all of which had a common theme. This was that lethal aspiration pneumonia had been deliberately induced by senior staff force-feeding patients. The method in all cases was that feeding beakers were filled with diluted puree and poured down patient's throats until they inhaled it. The evidence in all cases was flawed: There were no eye-witnesses, though in some cases if was claimed that "gurgling noises" had been heard from outside closed doors whilst patients were being fed. No post-mortems had been performed and the recorded causes of death did not fit with the accusations. The GP and care home records were of poorish quality for the times in question and the memories of other staff were that nothing out of the ordinary had occurred. No criminal prosecutions resulted.

Some 5% of people over 65 years of age receive community based care at home with many of them having some degree of cognitive deficit which normally progresses. All patients with dementia are very vulnerable adults who may be neglected or suffer financial, emotional, physical and sexual abuse. Abusers are more likely to be friends, family, and formal carers rather than complete strangers. However it is not uncommon for strangers to inveigle themselves into a vulnerable person's life, perhaps innocently at first and then take advantage of the situation. Financial abuse is covered under the criminal laws concerning fraud and theft. Physical abuse and neglect are covered by section 44 of the Mental Capacity Act of 2005, where a person in a position of trust ill-treated or neglected a person lacking capacity whilst under their care. To establish lack of capacity it needs to be proven firstly that at the time in question, there was an impairment/ disturbance in the functioning of the mind and brain which was either permanent (e.g. dementia) or temporary (e.g. delirium, drugs/alcohol) and then secondly that there was resultant lack of capacity.

The assessment of mental capacity is normally contemporaneous and task specific. In the absence of good evidence to the contrary there is a presumption of capacity. Such assessments are not the prerogative of psychiatrists and are well within the competence of most medical practitioners and psychiatric nurses, particularly so for those doctors and nurses who specialise in the care of elderly patients, many of whom will have evidence of cognitive impairment and/or dementia.

When neglect or physical abuse is suspected there is often a need to assess capacity in retrospect. In this event, the benchmark criteria for lack of capacity are:-

Firstly to establish whether the individual was unable to make a decision for themselves, owing to an inability to understand information relevant to the decision, or inability to retain, use, or communicate their decision because of an impairment of or disturbance in the functioning of the mind or brain. Sometimes the medical records are very poor indeed with no actual robust diagnosis other than vague reference to on-going "confusion". In that event, useful information can be gleaned from those in the "know" and interrogation of care records can be implemented to obtain as much evidence as possible about the abilities of individuals. Negative answers to the following questions (if due to mental reasons) give a good indication of general capacity sufficient to satisfy the courts:

a) Would the individual have the ability/capacity to identify risk and the ability to avoid it?

b) Would the individual have the ability to understand their condition?

c) Would the individual be able to live independently without assistance?

d) Would the individual be able to wash themselves?

e) Would the individual be able to clothe themselves?

f) Would the individual be able to feed themselves?

Some examples of criminal abuse I have assisted with include:

- Undue influence to cause a change to wills
- Stealing or pressurising someone to hand over money
- Physical assault causing actual harm
- Treating or teasing someone in a way that makes them feel threatened, belittled or embarrassed
- Sexual assault, both real and imaginary
- Neglecting someone's needs.

Before dealing with some specific cases the background of cognitive impairment and dementia needs to be explained in some detail.

Contrary to popular opinion, most old people, including the very elderly, have no significant cognitive impairment. Cognition is the process by which knowledge is acquired and includes perception, intuition and reasoning. Increasing age is however, associated with slower information processing and memory retrieval, but even this is not universal, and even when present, is not so severe as to interfere with day-to-day functioning. The perceived importance of information and its emotional associations will tend to aid memory storage and recall. Accuracy of recall is given preference over speed, but keeping track of more than one thing at a time and rapidly understanding complex material tends to become more difficult and can be further aggravated if vision and hearing are in any way impaired.

Some cognitive impairment is however commonly associated with ageing and for the most part is confined to memory loss which can be a frustrating nuisance. It is not necessarily so significant as to interfere with capacity, day-to-day function or independence. Deficits in language, understanding, logical thought processes and personality/ behavioural changes do not occur (those are the hallmarks of dementia). The condition slowly worsens with the vicissitudes of ageing but is not technically progressive like dementia. The mildest form, age associated memory impairment (also called the benign forgetfulness of old age) affects up to 40% of the over 65 age group and is characterised by self-perception of memory loss and a decline in objective memory tests as compared to younger adults with only 1% progressing to dementia each year. Mild cognitive impairment is a term used to describe a more severe form of memory loss which can often mimic the deficits in early Alzheimer's disease. About 10% of the over 65 age group have this condition with nearly 15% of them progressing to dementia each year.

Dementia by contrast, is a specific medical condition defined as an acquired global impairment of intellect, memory and personality, which is irreversible and progressive in nature causing impairment of and disturbance to the functioning of the mind and brain. This leads to a decline in the ability to perform daily activities, as well as to behavioural changes. It is also important to understand that the nature of dementing illness is such that it is not confined merely to memory loss. The personality often disintegrates, along with the ability to think logically and to understand what is happening around them. This can reveal itself in both irrational paranoia and excessive trust of a child-like nature. Long standing friendships can break down from paranoia and new friendships form which may be considered unusual by others. They lack resistance to outside pressures and may be readily manipulated and abused. The deficits often manifest themselves in abnormal behaviour because of a distorted perception of events from disordered reasoning. Alcohol consumption only makes matters worse. Common behavioural changes include: lack of motivation to provide self-care, wandering, disinhibition, resisting help and aggression.

Dementia is an umbrella term for a number of specific conditions. The commonest causes are Alzheimer's disease, Cerebral-vascular disease and a mixture of the two. Many sufferers (up to 50% of the very elderly) fail to receive a proper assessment and diagnosis and speculative diagnoses of the sub-types of dementia are often inaccurate. However dementia is routinely diagnosed accurately and clinically on the basis of deficits (below previous intellectual and educational levels) in memory, language, understanding, and logical thought together with personality and behavioural changes. These deficits can be measured to a degree and where not actually measurable collateral history from family members can be obtained. This may reveal aberrant behaviour, change in personality, and failure to cope with the straight forward activities of daily living. A typical history will include intermittent odd behaviour, a change in personality, forgetfulness and the inability to perform complex tasks or follow a complicated television play. Erratic driving, a history of losing keys, bus pass, spectacles, of burning saucepans, leaving gas fires on after bedtime are frequent concerns expressed by family usually denied by patients who have forgotten the incidents.

Although memory impairment is characteristic of dementia, the true extent of memory loss in dementia may be effectively disguised by a confabulatory response to questions. In effect, this is the painting in of the blank spaces in the memory with plausible responses. In the early stages of a dementing illness, it is possible, without performing specific tests of mental function, to assume that individuals are in full possession of their mental faculties. The observed continuation and/or progression of these deficits over at least 6 months is essential in avoiding misdiagnosis. Blood tests and brain scans assist in the diagnosis mainly by excluding other conditions rather than providing positive confirmation. The full extent of cognitive impairment is normally assessed by means of a mini mental state examination (MMSE), which is a set of well-validated simple questions/tasks, giving a maximum score of 30. Scores above 24 are consistent with the mild forms of memory loss discussed earlier. Scores below 24 are increasingly suggestive of significant cognitive impairment/early dementia. Scores below 20 suggest moderate dementia and those below 10 indicate advanced dementia. Scores below 16 are rarely compatible with unassisted independent living and increasing supervision becomes necessary as matters worsen. In a typical dementia of predominantly Alzheimer type, the score on the MMSE falls by 2 points, year on year as the dementia progresses. In dementia with a significant vascular component, progress continues but is much less predictable. Both relative stability for longish periods (of months or even a year) and sudden dramatic deteriorations may occur. In addition to the MMSE tests, more sophisticated tests such as the ACE-R may be used. A very simple AMT test of 10 questions can be used as a screening test for those admitted to hospital with acute illness.

Short term memory loss and inability to form new memory occurs early in the condition and there is progressive loss whereas long term memory is normally preserved. (Forgot what they did last week/month/year but vividly recall their childhood/wedding/Churchill's funeral etc.). Skills learned as young adults are retained for a long time. Musical memory and the ability to play the piano is usually very well preserved. Sewing skills are retained by females and men usually retain their "trade skills". They may wrongly appraise the need for their skill at any given time and use them inappropriately but perform some of the basics technically well. A demented plumber or electrician may start a job at home but forget why they were doing it and abandon it unfinished resulting in floods, fires or electrocution. Piano playing may be done inappropriately at night or the wrong thing sewn. Reminiscence therapy is a standard technique used to calm and raise the mood of dementia sufferers by encouraging people to use their skills under supervision. With the aid of props such as old newspapers or games people's moods can be lifted by reminiscing about the "good old days". Although technically speaking reminiscence therapy is manipulation, it is well-meaning and therapeutic.

Dementia and personal wealth are both increasing. Dementia and will making are awkward companions. This has led to more wills being contested after a testator's death. Such disputes over the distribution of the estate of a deceased person can be bitter, destructive of family relationships and very expensive. Rarely is there sufficient evidence of criminal activity to justify prosecution and aggrieved parties have to pursue matters in the civil courts for which there is rarely any legal aid (remember Jarndyce and Jarndyce, the expensive long drawn out fictional court case from the novel Bleak House by Charles Dickens). On over 40 occasions I have assisted both civil and criminal courts on aspects of testamentary capacity, mostly having been asked to give a retrospective opinion on testamentary capacity at the time the will was made. In such cases although the legal principles are clear the evidential problems can be significant. The normal scenario is that the will is considered to be grossly unfair and disputed. The grounds on which a will can be challenged are fraud or forgery, undue influence (bullying) and lack of testamentary capacity. Now and again someone with a perfectly valid reasoned will already in place and with a dementia (undiagnosed and medically unsuspected) is taken to a different solicitor by an opportunistic relative or friend and a new will executed favouring that individual. (In early dementia, close friends and relatives pick up the signs very early. They can keep the person away from doctors for the key time and beguile an inexperienced solicitor into considering that any minor problems in communication are due to sight and hearing deficits). After death that new will is then produced as the “trump card”.

Banks v Goodfellow test

The recent England and Wales High Court case of *Walker v Badmin* (2014) established beyond doubt that the long-held *Banks v Goodfellow* [1869 –70] LR 5 QB 549 test for testamentary capacity overrides the capacity test set out in the Mental Capacity Act 2005 (MCA) and remains the current test.

This case concerned the validity of the Will of John Banks. He was probably suffering from paranoid schizophrenia. He suffered from delusions that he was being persecuted by devils (they were sometimes visible to him) and also by a deceased local grocer. His will was challenged on the basis that he was insane and therefore unable to make a will. The will was found to be valid after trial by jury, before Brett J, at Cumberland Spring Assizes in 1869. On appeal, this judgment was confirmed unanimously by a panel of four appeal judges in Queen's Bench. The will was found to be valid, not influenced by his delusions, and deemed rational, being in favour of his only close relative (who also lived with him). In a strong and eloquent judgment, Cockburn CJ set out the following test of the capacity to make a valid will:

- A testator must understand the nature of the will and its effect. This does not require a full understanding of the legal terminology of the will, however a broad understanding of the will's effect is essential.
- A testator must have some idea of the extent of the property of which they are disposing this need not be an inventory which breaks down into an intricate detailed list, but the testator must appreciate the extent of their wealth.
- A testator must be aware of the persons for whom he would usually be expected to provide (even if he

chooses not to) and must be free from any delusion of the mind that would cause him reason not to benefit those people.

This would suggest there is an onus upon the will writer to determine the answer to these questions, and to comply with the criteria to establish testamentary capacity for people whose testamentary capacity might be called into question. A will writer ought to be prudent when taking instructions from a client that observations in respect of capacity are made from the outset and maintained throughout the process of completion of a will. Much litigation in the United Kingdom and elsewhere could be avoided if:-

- Solicitors had arranged for a will execution to be videotaped to demonstrate that they had asked the testator about his property and about his family, and that the contents of the testator's will had been gone through and fully understood.
- The witnesses to the will specifically swear or affirm an affidavit that the will was prepared under the supervision of an attorney and with the correct safeguards.
- Solicitors adhered to the "golden rule" by asking doctors to certify testamentary capacity (capacity for making a will) in potential testators at the time.

The Golden Rule

The law provides further guidance that should also be considered where a testator is deemed to be 'aged' or is seriously ill. The case of Re Simpson [1977] 121 SJ 224 provides that there is one golden rule that is to be observed, however straightforward the will and however tactless the suggestion, 'that the making of a will by an aged or seriously ill testator ought to be witnessed or approved by a medical practitioner who has satisfied himself of the capacity and understanding of the testator, and records and preserves his examination or findings.'

It is essential that a doctor asked to give an opinion on the testamentary capacity of a patient follows a procedure which is robust, conforms to expert opinion and is able to withstand critical scrutiny. Sadly this is either not done at all or else done to a poor standard.

The New Zealand case of *Woodward v Smith* involved a family member challenging the validity of changes made to the will of an elderly man after he had suffered a stroke. The Court of Appeal carefully described the test for testamentary capacity, and the correct process by which this should be carried out.

While it is for the court to decide whether a will is valid or not, a careful medical assessment, fully documented, at the time the will was made can be very helpful to the court, or remove the need for legal proceedings completely. Such an evaluation will also stand the doctor in good stead should the assessment of mental capacity come under the critical spotlight in a dispute between possible beneficiaries.

The reporting judge in the Woodward case approved of a paper published in the British Medical Journal, (Jacoby R and Steer P, 'How to assess capacity to make a will', *BMJ* 335:155 (2007) which recommended that doctors use the following process:

- Get a letter from the solicitor detailing the legal tests
- Set aside enough time
- Assess (according to standard medical knowledge) whether the patient has dementia

• Check that the patient understands each of the *Banks v Goodfellow* criteria, being:

a) The nature and effect of making a will

b) The extent of his or her estate

c) The claims of those who might expect to benefit under the will

The patient should not have a mental illness that influences making gifts in the will that would not otherwise have been made. Also:

• Record the patient's answers verbatim

• Check facts, such as the extent of the estate, with the solicitor

• Ask about and review previous wills

• Ask why potential beneficiaries are included or excluded

• If in doubt as to capacity, seek a second opinion from an experienced professional.

Parker v Felgate test

This test from 1882 is of relevance to doctors as it covers the law on intervening incapacity between giving the instructions for and the signing of (executing) the will. Someone ill, often in hospital, but with full testamentary capacity might summon a solicitor and give instruction on which basis the will is typed up. The law rarely works fast and often it is days later before it is available for signing in front of the witnesses by which time the patient may have deteriorated. In that event as long as they can recall that they gave earlier instruction and are signing the will based upon those instructions, the will is valid.

Cases of Contentious Probate

CASE 1 – I was asked to provide a retrospective report upon the likely testamentary capacity of an 85 year old lady, Mrs G, with reference to the Will she made at a time when there was unequivocal evidence of a background of self-neglect and short-term memory loss. Although a doctor was present when the solicitor took instructions for the new will and wrote a letter confirming her testamentary capacity, it was flawed by the absence of evidence that:

i) He had consulted her records beforehand

ii) He knew her well

iii) He knew of psychiatric concerns and pointers to cognitive impairment

iv) The absence of any Mini Mental State Examination even after he had noted that she needed prompting about her age and family relationships

My opinion was that without the doctor's letter indicating his contemporaneous assessment of her testamentary capacity, it would be my opinion that on the evidence, which I had seen, there was strong evidence of significant but unquantified cognitive impairment, sufficient to have interfered with her testamentary capacity and also to have rendered her vulnerable to undue influence, which she would have been unable to resist.

The evidence of the doctor was however potentially very strong, contemporaneous and weighty. As such, due regard must be given to this, It was up to the courts to decide as to whether his evidence was sufficiently robust to be relied upon.

CASE 2 – Mrs D, when approaching the age of 85 years of age, gave instructions for a change to her Will on 15/05/2007 and signed it on 29/05/2007. Her testamentary capacity at that time was questioned, on the basis of cognitive impairment, which subsequently became apparent during October and November 2007. Substantial lay evidence strongly suggested an abrupt decline from normal cognition after the summer of 2007 and there were no concerns expressed by anyone about how she was coping with her own needs, or caring for her dog prior to October 2007. Her solicitor, supported by his detailed contemporaneous notes, was very confident that she had testamentary capacity during May 2007 and that his confidence was sufficiently strong for him to ignore "The Golden Rule". He obtained no medical evidence of capacity. There were no medical records of her cognition for the time in question. There was however strong evidence for significant memory problems from November 2007, namely a MMSE score of 21/30, on 05/11/07 and a low ACE-R of 64 on 18/01/08. Her MMSE had fallen to 19/30 by 11/02/08. There was also a significant decline in her physical health and behaviour over this period. She had vascular risk factors and a CT scan of her head in February 2008 showed evidence of small vessel disease, with some age related atrophy.

I considered that, on the balance of probability, Mrs D retained testamentary capacity before and during May 2007 and lost it abruptly due to cerebral-vascular disease around October 2007.

CASE 3 – S D, when aged 86 years of age, gave instructions for her will on 5/8/2009 and signed it on 1/9/2009. On both occasions she was accompanied by a "friend" who, in contrast to previous wills, was named as the main beneficiary. I was asked to provide a retrospective report upon her likely testamentary capacity during that period. Robust medical records subsequent to June 2006 revealed the following:-

a) Request for a consultant psychiatrist, to perform a domiciliary visit on 04/07/07, at which time there were memory problems.

b) CPN records dated 06/06/07 recorded confabulation and a MMSE score of 17/30.

c) A further request for a consultant psychiatrist to perform a domiciliary visit on 22/01/09. The correspondence letters spoke for themselves in revealing memory problems, disorientation, and agitation and that she was not coping well at home with her personal hygiene and food hygiene. Specifically the psychiatrist did not think that she had the ability to deal with her own finances and queried her ability to understand the full implications of instructing for a lasting power of attorney.

d) Nine references to confusion/memory problems recorded by her general practitioner between March 2006 and August 2009 including the specific diagnosis of senile dementia in November 2007 progressing to that of severe dementia by 17/09/09.

I considered that S D lacked testamentary capacity before, during and after August 2009. I also considered that her dementia ought to have been obvious to those around her and ought to have been picked up by any solicitor acting with due diligence such as to prompt medical review. Collusion between the "friend" and the solicitor was suspected but not proven to the criminal standard. Nonetheless the solicitor was successfully sued for professional negligence.

Chapter Four

Financial Abuse

Many people with dementia are financially abused with their money being withdrawn from an ATM on a weekly basis by someone else. These cases either never come to light or, if they do, it frequently proves difficult to mount successful prosecution unless the sums withdrawn are excessive. In one case of mine, a ne'er do well grandson moved in with his grandfather who had early dementia and arranged substantial loans over the internet by posing as him. They opened a joint account from which he extracted the money. By the time it was discovered, the grandfather's dementia had advanced to such a degree that he was unable to make a reliable statement. The grandson maintained the position that everything was done at grandad's behest to give the young man a "helping hand". The CPS were unable, through lack of medical evidence, to prove lack of capacity to mount such a joint enterprise for the crucial times and he got away with it. Grandad died shortly afterwards and the debt died with him. The banks bore the loss. Few people are as audacious as DM in case 4 or as cunning as Y in case 5 whose plan, if successful, would have netted a serious sum and avoided inheritance tax!

CASE 4 – LP was a widow of 73 years with alleged dementia who was a talented musician. She was financially very well off and lived alone supported by a loose arrangement of various part-time paid carers. DM, a man in his 60's, first became involved with her as a paid carer in or around February 2014 and after he ceased being paid he continued to visit as a "friend". They shared musical interests. In September 2014 he took her on a trip to Sri Lanka. Under the pretence of taking her to the hairdressers they had rushed to Heathrow and boarded the pre-booked flight, having already packed her suitcase and hidden it in readiness. Her family reported her as missing and in due course the police/Interpol discovered her whereabouts and they were returned home. It soon became apparent that they had opened a joint bank account together. This had been topped up with substantial sums of her money which DM subsequently removed. DM had also discovered that her late husband still had money in a bank account in Sri Lanka and the reason for the trip was to access this resource. In due course DM faced charges of kidnap, fraud and theft and was convicted of theft at trial.

DM's defence was that they had planned everything together as a joint enterprise and that she had mental capacity.

The Crown's case depended upon proving her lack of capacity and I was asked to give an opinion upon the reliability of the diagnosis of dementia, its severity and the consequent likely mental capacity of LP. It was considered that, in view of the diagnosis of dementia, she would have lacked the capacity to have made the relevant decisions. Specifically my opinions were sought as follows:-

To deal with general issues regarding dementia by providing:-

- A summary of dementia i.e. its progression and effects
- Detail of what the visible and/or apparent effects of dementia and Alzheimer's would be to those who would spend time with the sufferer, i.e. had regular contact with them
- An explanation as to whether there is a reliable measurement/way of grading the level of a person's dementia and/or Alzheimer's. If so, what is it?

To deal with matters specific to LP by providing:-

- A summary of her development of dementia
- Detail of what the visible and/or apparent effects of her dementia would be to those who would spend time with the sufferer i.e. had regular contact with her;
- Comment upon what level her dementia had reached by 1st July 2013 when she, "received a score of 10". What does this score signify? What if anything can be concluded about her capacity from this score and how would this manifest itself to others?
- Comment on the assessments made by the health care professionals who had contact with her [It was suggested that on the 29th August 2014 a social worker, informed a witness that she "still had capacity to choose her friends"];
- What, if anything, could be concluded about her capacity from an observation of her being seen throwing items out of the window?
- Someone also stated, "I was also acutely aware that LP was so happy when DM was around and in her life." Was there any clinical support for a bond being formed by LP as a result of her condition(s)?

The records supplied included GP records from 2007 and correspondence from neurology and memory clinic attendance which were highly relevant and spoke for themselves. They were of excellent quality and her GP, who knew her well, provided a summary in statement form drawing attention to the increasing concerns about LP's mental state from June 2013. In chronological order I highlighted the following:-

- A recorded educational background that she initially entered university to study medicine but then switched to train as a physiotherapist

- In 2008 an MRI scan of her head showed evidence of small vessel cerebrovascular disease

- In March 2009 she was recorded as being agitated and confused; her MMSE score was 29/30. In April 2009 expressive dysphasia (problem in using language) was noted and a probable small stroke was diagnosed. A letter from a consultant neurologist in April 2009 described an MRI of brain as showing "significant small vessel changes-periventricular and subcortical"

- In February 2012 there were concerns about her driving safety and the DVLA were informed

- In March 2012 word finding difficulties, confusion and the previously recorded small vessel disease were noted

- The GP record summary recorded a diagnosis of Alzheimer's disease-aphasic variant for 2012 {The collateral evidence of her son, that she signed a power of attorney in June 2012, suggests she had capacity at that time}

- On 01/07/13 her MMSE score was 10/30. In August/September 2013 concerns about her alcohol consumption were noted, she had lost keys and worsening dementia was recorded

- By January/February 2014 she was in receipt of Donepezil therapy (a specific medication claimed to slow the progression of Alzheimer's disease). Her MMSE score was 11/30

- In February 2014 her need for carers 3x daily was noted with the added comment that she lacked insight as to why the carers came

- A note of the 28/09/14 described her arrival back from Sri Lanka at Heathrow airport. She was physically independent and mobile

- In September 2014 her GP formally recorded that she lacked capacity to make decisions about her welfare, financial or otherwise

- I noted that her repeat medications included medicines which could affect the mind. Lorazepam (sedative) 0.5 mg up to 4x daily; Donepezil (anti dementia) 5mg once daily and Citalopram (antidepressant) 10mg once daily. The doses prescribed were relatively low

- Other medications were Aspirin 75mg once daily, Felodipine, Bisoprolol, Simvastatin, Ramipril and Bendroflumethiazide. None of these were sedatives. Aspirin is normally given when there is vascular disease and risk of heart attack or stroke

Some 10 statements were also provided, all of which give different perspectives from both lay and professional backgrounds. I particularly highlighted and commented upon:

- The statement of HK dated the 12/09/14 noted deteriorations which she observed from November 2012. They included LP's disinterest in caring for herself and consequent lack of self-care without help and prompting from carers, the loss of inhibitions and excess alcohol consumption on occasions. I have noted that HK was also acutely aware that LP was so happy when DM was around and in her life **COMMENT-** consistent with reminiscence therapy. I have also noted her observations of LP when HK visited LP and saw her throwing items out of the window. These "snap shots" suggest a labile personality.

- The collateral evidence of her son, that she signed a power of attorney in June 2012, suggests she had capacity at that time.

- I also noted that it had been suggested that on the 29th August 2014 that a social worker informed a witness that LP "still had capacity to choose her friends". **COMMENT-** Dementia pre-disposes to poor decision making across the board from lack of logical reasoning/capacity. This includes choosing friends.

DM's defence was that they had planned everything together as a joint enterprise with her having mental capacity. His explanations and my comments thereon were:-

- The defendant suggested in his interview that the idea to go to Sri Lanka (August/September 2014) was LP's idea. **COMMENT.** In my opinion and on the basis of her diagnosis and reduced MMSE score of 11/30 in January/February 2014 LP would not have been capable of coming up with such a plan.

• The defendant stated in his third interview that he and LP "knew what they were doing" when they went to the airport as they had been planning it for weeks. **COMMENT.** In my opinion and on the basis of her diagnosis and reduced MMSE score of 11/30 in January/February 2014 LP would not have been capable of understanding such a plan.

• The defendant also stated, "when she didn't take her medication she was fantastic." **COMMENT.** I listed the medications and highlighted the ones with the potential to alter the mind. In my opinion had those medications been omitted short-term or the occasional dose omitted there may have been less sedation and she may have seemed more alert. Had they been omitted long-term the likelihood is that depression, agitation and worsening behaviour would have resulted. Had the other medications been omitted short-term or the occasional dose omitted this would likely have been inconsequential. Had they been omitted long-term the likelihood is that her physical health would have declined in due course.

• There were several letters said to have been read and approved/signed by LP. **COMMENT.** In my opinion and on the basis of her diagnosis and reduced MMSE score of 11/30 in January/February 2014 LP would not have been capable of understanding them and approving them.

There was video evidence (10 clips) found upon DM's iPad and my comments were requested. In my opinion her behaviour did not appear inappropriate and she appeared mostly relaxed and content particularly when playing the keyboard and piano. In the last video, seemingly taken in Sri Lanka, she appeared more alert and focussed. If that was the case possible explanations included the warmth and sunshine and/or the possibility that the medications with the potential to alter the mind had been omitted short-term. However the more plausible explanation was that she was happily remembering and recounting pleasant memories from her youth. Generally any questions posed about recent events were closed questions and required simple answers of the yes/no variety and there may have been some confabulation within her longer responses. Her long term memory and piano-playing skills seemed well preserved. Musical memory is well preserved in dementia. Nothing I saw in those video clips was inconsistent with dementia and nothing therein suggested full understanding of her current situation.

I gave my opinion as follows: Set against the background of higher than average educational attainment, the diagnosis of dementia, of sufficient severity to severely affect capacity, after June 2012 was increasingly robust and beyond any reasonable doubt after July 2013. {From the medical evidence of small vessel disease, the rapid onset and seemingly step-wise deterioration, it is likely that there was a significant vascular component. Technically she was likely to have had a mixed Alzheimer/vascular dementia}. The hard evidence for dementia was in the MMSE scores, the contemporaneous diagnoses by specialists and the lack of improvement. The supportive evidence by way of her need for care (due to disinterest and lack of planning, not physical dependency), personality and behavioural changes noted within the witness statements was compelling. Taking everything into account, the evidence for advanced dementia (an impairment/ disturbance in the functioning of the mind and brain) after July 2013 was unequivocal and robust. As such it was my further opinion that she would have lost her capacity for all but the most basic decisions on biological imperatives where the bar for capacity is correspondingly low – typically she would likely have retained capacity regarding choices of food etc. after July 2013 but lost it for the more complicated decisions. As such she would not have had the capacity to manage her financial affairs, decide on whether to make gifts, embark upon joint financial enterprises or understand the need for travel or agree to go abroad because:-

- She could not understand and retain the necessary information of relevance

- She could not use or weigh the information as part of the process of making a decision in respect of those matters, be they financial or travel matters

The absence of any defence medical expert in court to challenge my opinions spoke volumes. After some 3 hours giving my evidence in chief and subsequently being cross examined, the jury were convinced of her lack of capacity and this secured DM's conviction on the charge of theft and he received a custodial sentence.

<u>CASE 5</u> – JB was a very wealthy widower of 93 years who had a moderately severe vascular dementia though he remained fully mobile and for a time lived alone with escalating support. Both his two previous wives were dead. He had two natural children from his first marriage who were adults living many miles away who rarely visited. He also had two step-children who were adults living close by to whom he turned for support. An earlier will executed at a time of unequivocal capacity broadly bequeathed his assets to all four of these adults in equal shares. One step-son, Y, managed his affairs using a recently signed lasting power of attorney (LPA). His capacity to have signed

this was disputed by one of his natural children, W, who sought legal judgment in the High Court. The contemporaneous medical records were poor and whilst I thought his capacity may have been lacking I was unable to say that it was probably lacking. However the LPA in use had not been registered with the Court of Protection by solicitors acting for Y as it ought to have been. It was only registered after it was realised that W was taking matters to court. Things got messy and moved apace. JB was placed in care (before the LPA had been registered with the Court of Protection) and his house was put up for sale. The house was a substantial period property with extensive grounds in a prime location and probably worth upwards of £1.5 m. In fact it was put up for sale at £400k. No estate agent's board was put up and the only advert was a tiny notice in the estate agent's window which emphasised extensive damp and dilapidation. Within a few days someone, Z, offered the £400k and the sale process commenced and proceeded rapidly. Only then was the LPA properly registered with the Court of Protection. It became apparent to W that Z was a close friend of Y. It was alleged by W that the house was deliberately under-marketed and the deficits to the house were grossly exaggerated such as to facilitate a scam whereby Y and Z acting together would defraud the estate of £1m which they would later realise and share by a profitable re-sale. W pursued matters through the High Court and just in the nick of time blocked the sale.

Chapter Five

Alleged and Actual Assault

Whilst physical abuse is undoubtedly common, innocent individuals can be accused on flimsy evidence. Fortunately there are legal safeguards.

Unexplained bruising occurs commonly – estimating the age of a bruise is an inexact science at any age and particularly so in the elderly. Areas with good blood supply and poor supporting tissue, overlying a bony surface, bruise easily. In these areas, such as around the eyes, bruising can become apparent very quickly (within an hour) and then spread widely due to gravity. In tougher areas with good supporting tissue bruising will take much longer to become apparent and will remain more localised. Bruising to the upper arm can become apparent quickly but may take longer than an hour.

Elderly patients, but especially the very frail, are particularly prone to bruising, secondary to minimal and often extremely trivial trauma, due to the fragile nature of their capillaries. This tendency is significantly exacerbated in the event of a platelet or bleeding disorder or if they are on low dose Aspirin, Clopidogrel or Warfarin therapy. In any event, any bruising may spread widely due to the lax nature of the surrounding tissues. Any potential pattern from the agent responsible is lost quickly. Fragile skin may split from trivial blunt trauma, producing lacerations. Even in those patients who are bed fast, the head, forearms and legs are particularly prone to accidental trauma, often from trivial bumps against bedside furniture. Confused patients who wander are susceptible to bruising in the same areas either from falls or bumping into obstacles.

Elderly people often have poor appetites, especially in the presence of a dementing illness and many patients may be significantly deficient in vitamin C. In that event, the capillary walls may be even weaker than that which age alone would account for. Vitamin C is essential for collagen formation and deficiency even falling short of scurvy results in weakened capillary walls, with subsequent haemorrhage and bruising often occurring very easily and sometimes even spontaneously. The skin strength will also be reduced and will split more easily. As a consequence, trivial trauma may cause the sort of bruising which only significant trauma would cause in the young, whereas, major trauma from deliberate assault would usually cause marked bruising and often skin splitting in the elderly. It is against this background that I gave my opinions on the various injuries I was asked to review.

CASE 6 – D F, an 89-year-old lady, had been living alone at home, dependent upon carers who attended regularly. The carers accessed her house by use of a key, contained within a key safe. On Sunday the 27/06/10, her son found that she had several bruises upon her lower arms, which D F alleged had been caused by a carer, who had attended to her the previous day. It was later established that the carer in question was M who faced a charge of battery. She denied the offence.

Her defence team asked me to assist the courts by providing a medical report upon the bruising specifically commenting upon the following:

i) The potential cause of the bruising and whether this could have been the result of a deliberate assault, or whether more innocent explanations were possible

ii) Given her age and frailty, to give an opinion on the level of force which would have been required to cause this bruising and whether the elderly bruise more easily than the young

iii) Where possible, to give an opinion upon the reliability of the evidence of D F

I reviewed the following material:

i) Prosecution case summary

ii) Counsel's advice

iii) Defendant's defence case summary

iv) The complainant's ABE interview transcript

v) The complainant's medical notes, as served by the Crown

I noted:

i) That on the 18/06/10 her dietary intake was poor

ii) That she had sustained accidental falls, on both the 25/04/10 and the 19/05/10

iii) The absence of any formal mental assessment

iv) She was not in receipt of Aspirin or Warfarin

v) The GP's entry, on the 28/06/10, which described a laceration to her right forearm, bruising to the whole right forearm and some bruising of the left forearm. Dressings were recommended. The nursing record described a 4cm laceration to the left forearm on the 28/06/10 (different side recorded!)

vi) The police interview, a duration of 20 minutes, was conducted 4 weeks after the alleged assault. The transcript spoke for itself, in revealing basic discrepancies with regard to facts. Specifically, D F did not know her age, the current date or the date of the alleged assault. I noted that she said she reported the alleged assault to her mother and father

vii) All she could remember was a very basic thread, that she was pulled out of bed and put on the floor

My opinions were as follows:

• Despite the absence of a formal diagnosis of dementing illness the evidence from the interview would strongly suggest significant cognitive impairment, with the concomitant probability of there being a dementing illness. If that were the case, there was a likelihood that some, if not much, of her memory was false, being due to confabulation.

• In my opinion, given her age and likely fragile nature of her capillaries and skin, it was possible that the bruising and laceration were the result of trivial and normally inconsequential trauma. They could have resulted from appropriate manual assistance during position change. They could have been the result of a fall. They could of course be the result of assault.

• The only evidence for assault was the memory of D F, which, given the inconsistencies in her interview, must be considered to be flawed and unreliable, were it to be the sole evidence of alleged assault.

Her memory was the sole evidence and the charges were dropped.

CASE 7 – M D was an 89-year-old lady, who had only recently entered residential care due to her inability to properly care for herself. She had a background of atrial fibrillation, stroke with left sided weakness and evidence of cognitive impairment. Vascular dementia was suspected and a recent MMSE had been 22/28. The records of the home revealed recent uncharacteristic agitated behaviour with some violence to other residents suggesting that her vascular dementia was more advanced than the MMSE score would first suggest. Her medication included long-standing Aspirin 75mg daily. Diazepam 2mg x 3 daily had been increased to 5mg x 3 daily because of the violent behaviour and the potent antipsychotic drug Haloperidol 0.5mg 1-2 daily also prescribed. She was normally mobile with her walking aid (basically a metal walking stick with a tripod base) held in her right hand but she was falling with regular frequency. At least one of her falls was associated with falling on to her walking aid. She slept poorly.

One evening, she was admitted to hospital for further assessment of her confused behaviour and made allegations that she had been anally and vaginally raped in a toilet within the home. Bruising was noted. A police investigation was launched. Her family were distraught and baying for blood. She could not give specific details but the basic thread of the allegation had been reiterated over subsequent days. She was seen by an FME and photographs taken. Preliminary opinion was that the bruising was consistent with her allegations and samples including swabs were submitted for laboratory analysis.

The results were negative for rape and did not support her allegations. The police asked me to give an early opinion before distressing her with more invasive tests and before questioning under caution all males who had been in the vicinity of the home for the days before-including visitors, tradesmen, staff, doctors and deliverymen. Over 60 people had already been identified and the number was rising.

The photographs I reviewed spoke for themselves revealing widespread bruising to the face, arm and lower leg entirely consistent with falls over a number of days. The photographs of the genital area showed bruising which appeared to be more recent. Specifically there was linear bruising to the left and outside of the labia majora which extended backwards to the left outside of the anus over the ischial bone. Neither the vulva nor the anus showed evidence of any bruising or trauma and there was no evidence of bruising to the inner thighs which could have been expected if her legs had been forced apart.

In my opinion MD's memories and consequent allegations were very unreliable. They were most likely to be a false interpretation of something vaguely recalled due to a combination of her dementia exacerbated by sleep deprivation and sedative medication. Why she had those vague memories is open to speculation. She had seemingly led a very innocent and sheltered life. She could have experienced a distressing nightmare from recent medication which she misperceived as a real event. She could simply have misinterpreted the reason for her genital soreness.

The bruising to the genital area was, in my opinion, wholly inconsistent with anal and vaginal rape. Neither the vulva nor the anus showed any evidence of trauma.

Had she been raped I would have expected significant signs of trauma such as bruising, bleeding and skin tears to have been present in those areas.

The bruising to the genital area was of a linear nature and, in my opinion, wholly consistent with a fall to the right astride her walking aid such that the stem impacted into the left "crutch" and avoided direct contact with the vulva and anus. It could have arisen from a fall astride another linear object such as a bed rail. Other injuries noted were consistent with the series of well documented falls.

In summary, my opinion was that the medical evidence in this case strongly favoured innocent explanations for the cause of the injuries photographed. They were inconsistent with the rape of an elderly lady on Aspirin therapy. On the basis of her dementia and medications the allegations made by MD were at best unreliable and most likely false. They were not supported by the results of further laboratory tests. There was no objective evidence that any crime had been committed. The family were reassured that nothing untoward had occurred.

<u>CASE 8 – </u>W C was a man of 82, with dementia, living with his son D C. Serious injuries were first noted upon him, on 09/02/15. The external injuries were photographed and consisted of bruising to the face, left ear, left hand and wrist and a laceration below the left eye. There were also multiple left sided rib fractures (anteriorly) and a resultant left sided pneumothorax (collapsed lung). It was suspected that the injuries may have been the result of an assault at home perpetrated by his son D C. Specifically, I was asked to give an opinion as to whether his injuries were consistent with a fall/falls whilst walking a dog (as claimed by D C) or an assault.

W C was unable to give an accurate account of the events.

I noted lack of receipt of Warfarin, Aspirin or Clopidogrel therapy and that his clotting screen was normal. He appeared well nourished in the photographs (BMI recorded as 25).

I observed that frail people prone to falling rarely go outdoors unaccompanied or without a stick or similar walking aid and if they do, they tend to avoid dog-walking because of the obvious tripping hazards. Falls outdoors whilst walking dogs tend to occur in those who are younger and fitter. They normally fall from standing height and protect the head and chest by automatically extending the arms as they fall. Both wrists tend to be bruised or sprained and wrist fractures may occur. Bruising or grazing to at least one, or often, both knees is usual. Multiple rib fractures are rare unless there has been a collision with a lamppost, tree or wall. They tend to occur to the side or back of the rib-cage, not the front. Completely unilateral injuries are very uncommon indeed and ear injuries unusual. To injure the tissues around the eyes, from a fall, without there being some damage/bruising to the nose, is again very rare.

My opinion was that the pattern and totality of the injuries was entirely consistent with assault. They strongly suggested that the assailant was in front of a seated victim or above and to the right of one lying in bed. With assault occurring whilst standing I would have expected there to have also been some injuries to the back of the head or elsewhere from being knocked against obstacles or walls or being knocked to the floor. The pattern and totality of the injuries was not in keeping with a fall/falls in an individual taking Vitamin C and not taking medication which would enhance bruising. D C pleaded guilty on the advice of his Solicitor.

Sexual Offences

CASE 9 – AB was a well-preserved 70 year old lady with Alzheimer's dementia who was a long term resident in a dementia care facility. Physically she was fully mobile, attractive and looked younger than her years. With the help of staff she dressed tidily, sometimes wore make-up and often "flirted" with male staff in public. Staff noticed that her mood which was generally happy improved during early 2008 and she talked about her "special friend" who staff considered to be a delusional manifestation of her dementia. On one afternoon two staff members entered her room to find her having and seemingly enjoying sexual intercourse with a male, KA. The manager was fetched, followed by a social worker who contacted the police. It turned out that KA was a 54 year old male, of previous good character whose wife had "shut up shop" after the menopause. KA regularly visited the home in the company of his wife to visit her mother who was also resident in that home. He normally exchanged pleasantries and then sat in the corridor reading the paper for an hour or two until his wife was ready to leave. He admitted that his liaison with AB had begun months before and that they would discretely go to her room to have consensual sex as often as possible. KA was arrested and charged with rape on the basis that AB lacked the capacity to give informed consent compounded by the fact that KA must have known that she had dementia because that was the diagnosis of all the residents. AB was recorded as being upset immediately after they were interrupted but days later, when informally interviewed in my presence, she had little memory of the event though she did refer to wanting to see her "special friend" again. Because of her dementia the interview was of no evidential value and all I could say was that she had significant dementia and could not have given fully informed consent.

The law on capacity to consent to sex was and is far from straightforward mainly because sex is a biological imperative and the bar for capacity is correspondingly low. Capacity to engage in sex seems to hinge on whether they know that they can say "no".

I suspected that the Crown might have had difficulty in proving their case against a strong well-argued defence. In any event this was not tested in Court. KA's wife threw him out of the house, his children refused to have anything to do with him. He was laughed at in work. KA felt ashamed and embarrassed such that he pleaded guilty and received a custodial sentence.

Emotional Abuse

CASE 10 –Three care home workers from Lancaster were jailed in 2013 for ill treatment of elderly residents under their care. Whilst there were incidents of actual physical harm, much of the case centred on the bullying and teasing of 8 residents over an 18 month period. The motive for one appeared to be boredom which she relieved by mocking residents by regularly throwing bean bags at their heads. It was so obvious to the police that these residents had dementia that no-one had actually taken evidence to prove it. My involvement was merely to give an opinion on their lack of capacity retrospectively to ensure that the wall of evidence was unassailable.

Violence

CASE 11 – BN was a powerfully built mobile man in his 70's with significant vascular dementia, living at home with his wife who provided supervisory care with a formal carer visiting in the mornings to help him wash and dress. One morning the carer found him wandering in the locked house. His wife was dead. She was lying at the foot of the stairs, her neck was broken and there were multiple deep stab wounds in her chest. The carving knife was in her chest. Photographs of the hallway looked like they had been taken in a slaughterhouse. He was the sole suspect in her death. I was asked to examine him, address the evidence and give an opinion as to whether he was likely to have any memory of those events and whether he knew what he was doing and that it was wrong. Specifically I was asked my opinions on his mental capacity to be held responsible for his alleged actions, capability, ability to plead, potential danger to the public, condition at the time in question and his prognosis.

I found him to be in good physical health with significant dementia and a MMSE score of 16/30. He had no recollection of the events. Although what happened is unlikely to be known with certainty, it is probable that his actions were influenced by the dementia. His reasoning would have been clouded such that he could have falsely perceived a threat or sensed a provocative situation and lacked the self-control to prevent himself from violent over-reaction. He would not have been able to plan an assault. He is likely to have had some but limited understanding of what he was doing. He is unlikely to have foreseen the consequences of what he was doing or that it was wrong. He would have lacked full mental capacity. His physical capability to inflict injury was likely unimpaired.

In my opinion he was not mentally fit to plead. The cognitive impairment was such that he would be unable to follow a trial, he lacked memory of the key events (and could cause problems by confabulating a response), and was unable to respond to allegations and unable to instruct his legal team. He would not improve mentally and would deteriorate with time. Physical decline accompanies advanced dementia which then impacts upon life expectancy. He lacked the capacity to live independently in the community and was in need of some type of residential care. If so placed he was unlikely to be a threat to the general public. It was my further opinion that he was more of a risk to himself than to others. The most likely danger to others was that he could put himself in a dangerous situation, perceive help as threatening and violently react. He received a "hospital supervision order" from the courts but actually went to a dementia care nursing home.

Fitness to Plead – This depends on mental capacity.

Fitness to Stand Trial – This depends on physical health and whether the process of a trial carries a risk to health or even death. Doctors inexperienced in knowing what the courts require on this frequently make fundamental errors. Take for example the case of a mentally competent 88 year old man charged with historic sexual offences. Physically he has ischaemic heart disease, frequent angina, mild heart failure, and is on diuretics with concomitant COPD requiring long term oxygen. He is very poorly mobile with poor sight and hearing. He is fit to stand trial, though there may be practical problems which are not insurmountable. The courts could arrange for a nurse to sit with him in court to tend to his needs, monitor the oxygen, give him GTN, assist him to the toilet and make sure that that those matters upon which his sight and hearing depended were explained. The court could take frequent breaks to enhance his comfort. (Even if given a custodial sentence, the prison hospital could cope with his needs). By contrast a normally physically healthy individual struck down by acute "flu" or acute MI would be temporarily unfit to stand trial for the short period when either bed rest or active treatment was deemed essential.

Pathos

RW was a retired surgeon with advanced vascular dementia cared for at home by his wife, a retired nurse. He had been a kind gentle giant in his prime and remained physically fit. His behavioural problems caused her much pain:

- On one occasion she was leaving the house driveway in her car when he shouted out after her accusing her of stealing his wife's car. When she said she was his wife he denied it. He then pointed to their wedding photo indicating that it showed that his wife was that pretty woman not the "old bag" before him

- He rolled over in bed one morning and gently made love to her. She thought it sweet until he thanked her using her friend's name and then wrote a cheque in gratitude using their joint account cheque book!

Chapter Six

More on Dementia

The cruelty and misery of dementing illness is not confined to progressive cognitive impairment. There is physical decline, incontinence and progressive dependence due to progressive disconnection between brain and body. Normal reflexes are lost to be replaced by those seen usually in the new-born. In the latter stages it often accompanied by a disinterest in eating and drinking with concomitant weight loss and risk of dehydration. Quite simply dehydration results from inadequate fluid intake for the ambient environment. Demented patients are often reluctant to eat and drink and need encouragement to prevent dehydration and extra vigilance in monitoring the exact fluid intake/output to give early warning of potential problems to allow timely intervention if adequate oral intake cannot be maintained. Dehydration causes acute kidney injury and can be irreversible and lethal. Additionally dehydration even if only temporary worsens any predisposition to pressure sore development.

Patients with advanced dementia may not know that food is actually food and as a consequence not know what to do with it. In an advanced dementia the swallowing mechanism starts to fail, such that the patients are unable to coordinate the act of swallowing with the risk that food and especially fluid, is aspirated into the lungs. This potential to choke often frightens patients, leading to further reluctance to eat and drink. As a result, death in dementia is frequently from an aspiration pneumonia and usually accompanied by terminal weight loss and often dehydration. Artificial feeding with tubes is generally considered to be inappropriate, owing to the terminal and progressive nature of the underlying neurological illness. Furthermore insertion of a PEG tube involves an operation, which although small, carries a surprisingly high complication rate. Nasogastric tube insertion is safer but they can inadvertently be placed in the airway. All tubes may be pulled out by confused patients and serious problems arise if a PEG tube is pulled out. Repeatedly replacing pulled out nasogastric tubes is distressing and the risks of accidental placement in the airway increase. Nasogastric tubes can be anchored in situ with a "bridle" but if attempts are then made to pull them out serious trauma results. Tube feeding in any event does not protect from aspiration of saliva. Without regular eating and drinking and even with optimal mouth care saliva carries bacteria which can cause lethal pneumonia. Any regurgitation of the stomach contents (filled by tube feeding) will also produce aspiration pneumonia.

CASE 12 – When the Mental Capacity Act first came into force some eager lawyers were keen to be at the forefront of securing convictions. ET, a care home resident with dementia, died in 2008 in a grossly emaciated state. Her BMI of 13 suggested starvation. Her recorded nutritional intake suggested food intake of a tenth of her daily requirement. There was unequivocal evidence of dementia and the cause of death was bronchopneumonia brought on by malnourishment. The trial went ahead but “cracked” when the carers convinced the court that they had tried extremely hard indeed over many weeks to get ET to eat and drink. She consistently refused. The carers accepted that they recorded what she took in nutritionally but with hindsight should have recorded repeatedly what she was offered and refused. My evidence on the natural history of dementia in respect of food and drink intake assured acquittal.

CASE 13 – PS and JR were two elderly men who brawled in the street, resulting in the hospitalisation of JR with some relatively minor abdominal injuries. PS was arrested and charged with assault causing actual bodily harm. On-going pain led to suspicion of a splenic injury which was excluded by exploratory abdominal surgery under general anaesthesia. Unfortunately JR had a bad chest (COPD) and required a post-operative spell in ITU during which time a PEG feeding tube was inserted through his abdominal wall into his stomach. In due course he was transferred to a ward and seemed to be on the road to full recovery. The PEG tube remained in use to boost his nutritional intake. At 8am on a Saturday morning the D grade staff nurse on duty gave JR his routine PEG feed. Within an hour he complained of severe generalised abdominal pain. Peritonitis was diagnosed after prompt medical review but he was dead by lunchtime. The PEG tube had come out of the stomach but was within the peritoneal cavity-the feed had gone straight into that cavity and caused his death. {There are basic bed-side checks which ought to pick up a dislodged PEG tube before feeding is commenced.} PS was now charged with manslaughter. The D grade staff nurse made an exceptionally detailed police statement setting out how she had followed the text-book procedure bed-side checks in painstaking detail – she over-egged it. The ward at the time was busy and short-staffed such that most professionals who read her statement considered that she had cut a few corners and not followed procedure to the letter.

The defence of PS centred on claiming that the giving of the PEG feed without due diligence amounted to a **"novus actus interveniens"** i.e. a new intervening act which broke the chain of causation. I looked at this for the defence but felt that the timescale of an hour between the starting of the feed and complaint of pain suggested that the tube dislodged after her check and sometime after the feed had been started.

The judge ruled that the chain of events was unbroken in that JR would not have had a PEG inserted absent the assault and the D grade staff nurse had almost certainly acted correctly. PS was found guilty of manslaughter.

Naso-gastric tubes

These are fine bored soft feeding tubes inserted up the nose and then down the oesophagus into the stomach. Sadly some end up in the trachea, bronchi and lung. Putting feed into the lung causes severe pneumonia which is often lethal. X-ray will confirm correct positioning – but only for the instant when the x-ray was taken – the tube may have moved since. Many doctors of my generation were taught the "whoosh test" to check correct positioning before feed commencement –shoot air from a syringe down the tube and listen over the upper abdomen with a stethoscope for the sound of the air arriving in the stomach. THIS IS DANGEROUSLY

INACCURATE and condemned in all guidance for 10 years. (Yet it was done for years after red-flagged guidance was issued and may still be used). A patient safety alert was issued in 2005 but had to be re-issued in 2011 when it became apparent that there had been 21 deaths and 79 cases of harm due to feeding through nasogastric tubes misplaced in the lung often the result of x-ray misinterpretation. The only safe recommended bed-side check before each and every feed is to aspirate gastric fluid and confirm with pH paper (not litmus paper) that the acidity is such that it could only be from the stomach.

Cause of Death

The determination of cause of death is predominantly the territory of pathologists. However, sometimes the clinical perspective is more relevant in establishing the chain of events leading to death.

CASE 14- The prosecution's case for proving causation of death by dangerous driving hinged entirely on expert medical opinion. The pathologists and I disagreed. The established facts in this case were:-

- MH was a lady of 74 years. She had significant physical co-morbidities with bronchiectasis and previous minor strokes. She was a current smoker. Severe generalised arteriosclerosis was identified at post mortem. However, functionally she was mobile independently outdoors and the GP records provided no evidence to suggest she was very short of breath and no evidence of recent or recurrent chest infections during the year prior to the accident.

- She was a pedestrian, struck by a slow moving car on a Saturday shortly before 7 am at which time she was up and about, dressed and returning on foot from the local shop. She sustained a cut to her leg and bruising.

- Accompanied by her daughter, she walked into the local minor injuries unit at around 8 am. A large haematoma and "V-shaped" laceration to the outside of her right leg were identified, cleaned and dressed.

- The Community Staff Nurse attended MH at her home on the following Wednesday (in the morning) where she cleaned and dressed the injuries. She had been much less active following the injuries as she had been advised to "rest up" and stop smoking to improve healing. Her mobility declined and she became dependent upon others for washing, dressing, housework and shopping.

- By 22.19 hours on the Wednesday the records indicated the situation as "She is in bed… was found cold and clammy and rattly chest, on lots of medications, strokes in past. She is coming in and out of consciousness" and advised to call 999.

- From the hospital records I particularly highlighted:

a) The robust diagnosis of a left sided pneumonia with chest x-ray evidence of consolidation and the typical clinical signs of breathlessness, increasing respiratory rate, low oxygen levels and raised white cell count

b) The absence of abnormalities on her head CT scan. Also, Her ECG was unremarkable

c) There was an initial response to antibiotics and fluid resuscitation with improvement by 12 pm on the following day but this was short-lived. Despite on-going active treatment she deteriorated and continued to steadily decline thereafter, until she died 10 days after the injury.

As is normal practice with death from possible crime two pathologists were involved. Both agreed that the cause of death was:

1a Left sided Bronchopneumonia

1b Cerebrovascular disease, and soft tissue injuries due to road traffic collision

The problem was that whilst on the balance of probability they agreed that she would not have died at the time she did, had she not suffered the soft tissue injuries they were reluctant to commit to the degree of certainty which the CPS required.

I was asked to review the evidence and give a specific opinion, from my perspective as a geriatrician as follows: "Could I be sure that the injuries were a cause of death, meaning not the main or principal cause but a contributory cause which is more than trifling?"

I set out my argument as follows:

- MH was a 74 year old lady. As such UK actuarial tables (produced by the Office for National Statistics) would give an average future life expectancy to be of the order of another 16 years. However she was far from average with significant co-morbidities which would warrant a discount on that average of some 80% such that survival beyond 3-4 years would have been very unlikely. A vascular or respiratory death was highly likely in due course and could have occurred before 3 years.

- MH was active outdoors. She had been up, dressed and out to the local shop before 7 am on the day of the accident. To a geriatrician that implies a reasonable degree of fitness and that she felt well. This would not suggest that she was dependent or that there was a steepening trajectory of decline. Her death was very unlikely to be imminent unless she suffered a sudden vascular demise.

- There was evidence of bronchiectasis and on-going heavy smoking. Bronchiectasis involves the dilatation of the smaller air passages in the lung which can be patchy or localised. It can be minor or extensive. Her bronchiectasis did not appear to have been extensive or problematic whilst she was active. Lung secretions accumulate in the dilated areas and if not cleared frequently they can become infected and result in pneumonia. Keeping active and mobile assists expectoration and smoking the first cigarette of the day will often precipitate a coughing bout which will also assist secretion clearance.

- Most geriatricians are all too familiar with the serious consequences of even short periods of immobility upon the well-being of older patients. Rest for even a day or two usually results in some muscle weakness, progressing to reluctance to walk and ultimately to muscle wasting which impedes a return to the previous levels of mobility without some active rehabilitation. Injuries to the lower limb are particularly devastating in this regard and can quickly set in train a vicious circle of progressive functional decline, escalating dependency on others and even precipitate nursing home placement. Pneumonia is a common complication of reduced mobility in those with pre-existing chest conditions especially if bed-rest is taken to elevate an injured leg to reduce swelling.

• The risk of developing pneumonia can be estimated on a scale of 0-5 according to residual mobility where 0 represents baseline risk and 5 the highest risk. If she had maintained mobility within her home unaided and mobilised frequently her risk would have been low (1). Had she mobilised only when someone was available and willing to assist, her risk would have been (2). Had she been in too much pain to have walked even with assistance and spent most of her time sitting upright in a chair her risk would have been (3). Had she been in too much pain to have walked even with assistance and spent her time lying back in a reclining chair with her leg elevated her risk would have been (4). The greatest risk (5) would have resulted from bed rest. Sedative analgesia, even over-the-counter codeine, would have further heightened these risks of developing pneumonia.

• The accident occurred on a Saturday at or around 06.45 hours. Although she was able to walk immediately thereafter, she reduced her mobility and activities and smoking under nursing advice entirely due to the injuries. Within 5 days she had taken to bed and pneumonia had set in. This was a very short time-frame.

I gave my opinion as follows:-

• There was no reason to suppose that the death of MH was imminent. There was no reason to suppose that pneumonia would intervene whilst she was mobile. I was sure of this beyond reasonable doubt.

• The injury to her leg compromised her mobility and heightened her risk of developing pneumonia. I was sure of this beyond reasonable doubt. How immobile she became is a fact for the courts, not experts, to determine.

I have set out on a 0-5 scale how the risk would have risen with increasing immobility.

- In my opinion MH died of pneumonia set in train over a short time-scale by a decline in mobility. I was sure of this beyond reasonable doubt.

- I considered the likelihood of this pneumonia being entirely co-incidental and unrelated to the step-down in mobility from the injuries and could not rule it out as a remote possibility. The wise physician knows that the words “never” and “always” are best avoided in medicine. Taking into account the absence of susceptibility to actual frequent chest infections previously whilst she was mobile, the strong causal link between reduced mobility and pneumonia and the very short time-frame between the step-down in mobility and onset of pneumonia, I was sure beyond reasonable doubt that the pneumonia was not co-incidental.

- She would not have died when she did or how she did had she not sustained those injuries. I was sure of this beyond reasonable doubt. I was therefore sure beyond reasonable doubt that the injuries were a cause of death in the sense of meaning that whilst they were not the main or principal cause of death they were a contributory cause which was more than trifling.

The defence tried to exclude my evidence on the grounds that causation of death was for pathologists, not geriatricians, to determine. When the judge determined that the jury ought to hear my evidence the accused, having taken legal advice, entered a guilty plea and received a non-custodial sentence.

<u>CASE 15 –</u> JS was a 50 year old man, undergoing regular renal dialysis three times weekly, following a failed renal transplantation. There was a background of

ischaemic heart disease, hypertension, depression and he was a reformed alcoholic. He lived alone but did not take good care of himself, living under unkempt and squalid conditions but was a regular attender for his dialysis programme. He was not in receipt of immunosuppressive therapy.

He failed to attend for dialysis at 18.45 hours on the XXX as arranged. The staff nurse rang his mobile phone, which rang but no answer was obtained. She left a message on his voicemail service and tried again at 19.20 hours and yet again at 20.20 hours. At 21.27 hours she contacted the police, requesting that they attend urgently to check all was well. They did not attend that day, but upon attendance on the morning of the 21/09/06, he was found to have already died. Post mortem examination revealed an extensive and well-established right sided pneumonia, together with bilateral pulmonary oedema. Cause of death was given as:

1a)Pneumonia

2) Hypertensive heart disease

The failure of the police to attend was reported to the Professional standards department who needed to establish whether this delay contributed to death. They asked me to provide an opinion as to when death was likely to have occurred and as to how long his pneumonia would have taken to cause his death.

Having spoken to the pathologist who confirmed the extensive nature of the pneumonia, which was responsible for his death, it was my opinion that this had probably taken in excess of 48 hours to become that established. Owing to his co-morbidities he would have been prone to pneumonia, had little reserve to fight infection and any pneumonia would have advanced at a rapid pace. In my opinion, the probability was such that death had already occurred by 19.00 hours on the 20/09/06, which would have accounted for him failing to have answered his mobile phone. There is a possibility that at that time, he was just alive but unconscious, but under the circumstances of his medical background and the extensive nature of the pneumonia, it was unlikely that he would have responded to medical treatment.

Medication Errors

Such errors are surprisingly common but rarely consequential. However the lay public will often pursue legal redress with great vigour. I include two cases from the extremes of the spectrum:

CASE 16 – WT, a 91 year old man with vascular dementia, in a care home for respite, received another service user's medication at 17.00 hours on 14/04/12, instead of his Lactulose 15mls and Gabapentin 100mg due at that time. He actually received Adcal, Ranitidine and Arthrotec. The mistake was noticed immediately and his GP was informed. The advice given to the staff by the GP was recorded as close monitoring and that it may cause some diarrhoea. The contemporaneous GP records are silent but briefly refer retrospectively to the incident in a short entry of 27/04/12. It was alleged by his family that this error had long term consequences to his health and advanced the date of his death. They pursued this case on a "no win, no fee basis" {Solicitors are normally very astute about taking on no win no fee cases. They have a very high threshold of some 80% expectancy of success before agreeing to act}. I suspect that mention of diarrhoea on the death certificate wrong footed them here. His death in Hospital on 09/08/12 was certified as being from:

1a) Hospital Acquired Pneumonia

2) Vascular Dementia, C. difficile diarrhoea

Review of his records revealed that loose stools were recorded subsequent to the medication error with the last episode at 06.00 hours on 15/04/12. He appeared well and was returned home by Taxi at 11.30 hours. Upon return home there was a large episode of faecal incontinence which resulted in his return to the care home that day for monitoring. When seen by his GP on 16/04/12 he was considered fit to return home. According to the notes made by his family he returned home on 19/04/12 but was subdued and had little appetite. This persisted until 22/04/12 when he complained of pain and the inability to pass faeces after spending 4 hours on the toilet. The district nurse was contacted, visited, checked him over and after discussing matters with the "on-call" doctor requested an emergency ambulance. He rapidly deteriorated as follows:-

- **Admission 22/04/12 to 20/06/12** The initial diagnosis was constipation/faecal impaction which responded to a suppository. He was incontinent of urine and had a fall on 23/04/12 at 19.45 hours and hurt his left shoulder. X-ray followed and orthopaedic review excluded significant injury and recommended no action. He remained confused and incontinent of urine. By 26/04/12 he was coughing and there was chest x-ray evidence of right lower lobe opacification. Antibiotics were given for a chest infection. His mobility faltered due to a right knee effusion considered to be due to gout but improved following aspiration. MRSA colonisation of the throat was noted.

By 03/05/12 he was considered "fit for discharge" but intervening drowsiness thwarted this. A CT scan of his head showed only age-related changes and small vessel disease. A course of Tazocin antibiotics was given for suspected sepsis from 08/05/12 followed by Meropenem from 10/05/12 to 13/05/12. Pulmonary oedema/fluid overload was evident on 14/05/12 and diuretics were given. He was catheterised, with more Meropenem given as cover for infection. By 24/05/12 he was stable and apyrexial and his catheter had been removed. Nose bleeding occurred and he was seen by ENT and settled. He remained medically stable during June and received rehabilitation but his mobility had not returned to that of early April. He was discharged on 20/06/12.

- **Admission From 21/06/12** Readmission on 21/06/12 was precipitated by confusion, disorientation, loss of co-ordination and visual hallucinations. A course of Trimethoprim for suspected urinary tract infection was given and completed on 27/06/12. Diarrhoea on 29/06/12 prompted stool analysis confirming C Diff positivity on 30/06/12. Metronidazole was started with addition of Vancomycin following bacteriological advice. Despite episodic diarrhoea he remained stable and participated with rehabilitation until a fall on 13/07/12. 2-3 right sided rib fractures were evident on the chest x-ray and analgesic patches given. Gentamicin was given from 16/07/12 following dip-stick suspicion of a urinary tract infection. A detailed appraisal on 19/07/12 noted his decreased alertness, bed-bound status and on-going infection and considered it unlikely that he would recover sufficiently to return home safely. He subsequently stabilised and improved slightly until developing a right sided chest infection on 27/07/12. Clarithromycin was given and Vancomycin continued following more bacteriological advice. His chest improved initially but loose stools persisted. On 06/08/12 he deteriorated suddenly with a raised heart rate, raised respiratory rate and reduced consciousness. An aspiration pneumonia was suspected, Tazocin commenced and he received chest physiotherapy. Despite on-going active treatment he deteriorated, developed a metabolic acidosis and died at 03.45 hours on 09/08/12.

With reference to the British National Formulary I noted the content, the uses and side effects of the medications Adcal, Ranitidine and Arthrotec which were:-

- **ADCAL** – This is a chewable tablet containing Calcium Carbonate (chalk) normally given for osteoporosis. Side effects are rare but include unspecified gastrointestinal disturbances.

- **RANITIDINE** – This is an H2 antagonist which reduces gastric acid production. Side effects are rare but include diarrhoea.

- **ARTHROTEC** – These are combination tablets given for arthritis containing Diclofenac {a non-steroidal anti-inflammatory drug (NSAID)} and misoprostol {a prostaglandin analogue which can both heal gastric/duodenal ulcers and prevent NSAID-associated ulcers}. Side effects from Diclofenac and misoprostol are rare but diarrhoea is included as a side effect of both.

I also observed that many of the hundreds of medications listed in the BNF include either unspecified gastrointestinal disturbances or diarrhoea as potential side effects from long term (months) or even short term (days-weeks) usage. Actual side-effects sufficiently severe to necessitate cessation of medication are rare but normally resolve upon cessation. It is exceptionally unusual to the point of being vanishingly rare for a one-off dose of any of the medications listed in paragraph 6 to cause problematic diarrhoea at all. Even in the very unlikely event that diarrhoea occurred from a one-off dose it would resolve within a day or two as those medications are cleared from the body quickly. Missing single doses of regular medication such as Lactulose 15mls and Gabapentin 100mg is very rarely consequential even over the period before the next regular dose is given.

My opinion, supported by the weight of contemporaneous evidence, was that this man's loose stools/faecal incontinence in April 2012 were due to constipation and resultant overflow incontinence, not diarrhoea.

I carefully considered the events of 14/04/12 and whether the incorrect administration of the medications or the omission of his normal medications had any adverse effect and whether there was any way that they could have caused or contributed to any decline. My opinion on this was unequivocal, that the events of 14/04/12 had no adverse effect whatsoever either of short or long term nature. They did not cause his loose stools, did not cause his constipation, did not cause any suffering and did not precipitate his hospital admission or advance his death.

It was my further opinion that his terminal decline during his final 4 months of life was natural and typical of the last months of someone of his age with vascular dementia. His hospital treatment was in accord with acceptable practice throughout.

CASE 17- M E, an 81 year old lady with pre-existing dementia received Amisulpride in doses greatly in excess of that prescribed and recommended whilst in respite care at a care home during November 2011. It is alleged that, as a consequence, her dementia was aggravated and advanced. Specifically M E was being prescribed Amisulpride liquid (100mg/ml) in a dose of 0.25mls (25mg) at night. The letter of 07/01/12 from the home and the minutes of the safeguarding case conference spoke for themselves in noting that she actually received 25 mls (2,500 mg) on the 22nd and 23rd November 2011, 2.5 mls (250mg) on 24th November, none on 25th and 26th November (omitted owing to sleepiness) and then 2.5 mls (250mg) on 27th November. She was admitted to Hospital on 28th November 2011 with drowsiness, unresponsiveness and reduced mobility. As evidenced by the discharge letter of 20/12/11, her baseline of mobility was never regained and she required a hoist for transfers. She was discharged to long term care at another home. In addition to seeing and examining her at her current home on 18/02/13 and interviewing both her husband and the nursing manager, I was provided with a bundle of material approximating to 300 pages containing her general practitioner records and hospital correspondence therein together with the background information.

With reference to the British National Formulary guidance on the prescription of atypical antipsychotic drugs such as Amisulpride, I highlighted the following:

- That they should be used with caution in patients with cardiovascular disease and with great caution in the elderly. Initial doses in the elderly should be reduced (to half the adult dose or less) taking into account factors such as the patient's weight, comorbidity and concomitant medication. The maximum daily dose of Amisulpride is 1200mg (and that is for youngish adults with acute psychoses). The dose should be reduced to half in the event of renal impairment (eGFR between 30 and 60).

• That dizziness, postural hypotension (especially during initial dose titration), weight gain and extrapyramidal signs (mimicking Parkinson's disease) are all recognised side effects.

It was against this background that I gave my opinion.

In view of this lady's significant mental and physical decline by June 2011 her prospects of remaining at home, cared for solely by her husband, for the very long term were poor. However she was receiving thoughtful proactive care and both her needs and those of her husband were being met with a gradually escalating care package. On the balance of probability, if she had continued her previous trajectory of decline and received concomitantly escalating support, her need for long term Nursing Home care would not have arisen before the end of 2013/ early 2014.

In my opinion, the administration of extremely high and totally inappropriate doses of Amisulpride was incompetent and negligent (all but a tiny dose was contraindicated by her renal impairment, age and cardiovascular disease). This acutely stepped down her mental and physical abilities. The exact mechanism is uncertain. She may have had an element of cerebrovascular disease making her very sensitive to reduced cerebral blood flow in which case any hypotension could have caused brain damage. The extrapyramidal signs were consistent with direct Amisulpride toxicity. It is likely to have been the result of more than just simply a period of around a week of drug induced sleep associated with lack of any exercise and mental stimulation. By whatever mechanisms, my firm opinion was that it set in train a series of unfortunate consequences, as follows:

- She became very sleepy and by the time she was hospitalised she was unresponsive. Not only was the opportunity for both her and her husband to benefit from the respite period lost but she was also made significantly worse.
- The consequence of this was a dramatic and permanent deterioration in her physical abilities which precipitated an otherwise unnecessary hospital admission and ruined her prospects of returning home. She never regained her previous function such that she entered permanent care some 2 years earlier than could have been reasonably envisaged.

Care of the dying Pathways

The use of "Care of the dying Pathways" has become controversial. The Liverpool Care Pathway (LCP) was developed for widespread use from the experiences of those dealing with terminally ill patients in Hospices. It provided a clear concise set of guidelines to ensure that dying patients did not suffer through mismanagement and pointless over-treatment. Prior to 2013 these pathways were commonly used when it was apparent that the life of a patient was drawing to a close. They had Government backing and such pathways enshrined the best principles of practice to ensure that death was as peaceful as possible by concentrating on symptom relief and not pursuing irrelevant medical actions. Following a furore of media attention during 2013 the Government withdrew its backing. Where these pathways had "bad press" it was usually the case that they were either inappropriately commenced, or poorly delivered or done without informing the next of kin. It was the implementation of the pathways, not their principles, which were criticised. Recent polls have revealed that a substantial majority of Doctors would still wish for their own terminal care to be delivered according to the principles of these pathways. They do not hasten death but they do not prolong the process of dying either. (It is not uncommon for the pathway principles to be varied, paused or cancelled according to patient need and progress). Those principles of good end of life care still apply, are used regularly and are considered to represent "best practice". All death causes upset to family members but it is especially so when a relatively and seemingly fit person develops an acute illness followed by fluctuant though progressive deterioration. This can cause a serious mismatch of expectations between professionals and family. Sometimes delaying the implementation of care pathway principles for a few days allows time for views to converge but the interest of the patient must always come first. Any delays primarily for the benefit of family should only be done if not detrimental to the patient's best interest.

Cardio-Pulmonary Resuscitation.

Contrary to popular opinion (often gleaned from TV medical soap operas) successful resuscitation after cardiac arrest is much less than 50% in those of middle age with little co-morbidity. Over 75 years of age in the presence of multiple co-morbidities success is vanishingly small, often very short-lived (minutes /hours/days) and usually accompanied by serious brain damage especially if cerebro-vascular disease co-exists.

If attempted it is almost always futile and can turn a peaceful impending death into a distressing drama. Whether to attempt it or not is ultimately a medical decision. It is best practice to discuss matters with the patient or next of kin (if the patient lacks capacity) and inform them of the reasons why a DNAR (Do Not Attempt Resuscitation) order is appropriate. Because this sounds a negative act, it is sometimes better to introduce the topic in a less negative manner using the acronym AND (Allow Natural Death). Doctors are under no obligation to perform futile treatments which might not be in the patient's best interests. Neither the patient nor next of kin can demand resuscitation if it is medically inappropriate.

Chapter Seven

Gross Negligence – Manslaughter

Manslaughter is the unjustifiable, inexcusable, and intentional killing of a human being without deliberation, premeditation, and malice. Manslaughter is a distinct and lesser crime from murder. The essential distinction between the two offences is that malice aforethought must be present for murder. On conviction for manslaughter, sentencing is at the judge's discretion, whereas a sentence of life imprisonment is mandatory on conviction for murder.

Manslaughter can be either voluntary or involuntary. The main difference between the two is that voluntary manslaughter requires an intent to kill or cause serious bodily harm while involuntary manslaughter does not.

Voluntary Manslaughter

Voluntary manslaughter consists of an intentional killing that is accompanied by additional circumstances that mitigate, but do not excuse, the killing. The most common type of voluntary manslaughter occurs when a squabble or fight goes wrong and the defendant is provoked to commit the homicide. It is sometimes described as a heat of passion killing. If adequate provocation is established, a murder charge may be reduced to manslaughter.

Involuntary Manslaughter

Involuntary manslaughter is the unlawful killing of another human being where the accused did not intend to cause death or serious injury but caused the death through recklessness or criminal negligence. Recklessness is defined as a blatant disregard for the dangers of a particular situation. The absence of the intent element is the essential difference between voluntary and involuntary manslaughter. Generally there are two types of involuntary manslaughter:

(1) Unlawful-act manslaughter.

An example of this would be dropping a stone off a bridge which then hits a person's head, killing him. Since the intent is not to kill the victim, but simply to drop the stone, the *mens rea* (guilty mind) required for murder does not exist because the act is not aimed at any one person. But if in dropping the stone, there is a good chance of injuring someone, the person who drops it will be reckless.

(2) Criminal-negligence manslaughter.

Under English law, where a person owes a duty of care and is negligent to such a degree that the law regards it as a crime (namely the person has been grossly negligent) and that person causes the victim to die, he may be liable for gross negligent manslaughter. The specialist CPS units in London and York determine whether charges are brought. The defendants in such cases are often people carrying out jobs that require special skills or care, such as doctors, teachers, police or prison officers, or electricians, who fail to meet the standard which could be expected from a reasonable person of the same profession. {Some 40-50 doctors have been charged with manslaughter since 1990 – the same number as in the previous 200 years. The chances of conviction for those taken to court is less than 50%. The growing number of charges seems to reflect a need for "vengeance/retribution". Behind the scenes there is often a relative in denial of human mortality}. Gross negligence manslaughter involves the following elements:

- The defendant owed a duty to the deceased to take care;
- The defendant breached this duty;
- The breach caused the death of the deceased;
- The defendant's negligence was gross, that is, it showed such a disregard for the life and safety of others as to amount to a crime and deserve punishment.

The law on this as regards doctors was fine-tuned over the years with the Adamako case from 1994 establishing the current law. John Asare Adomako appealed to the House of Lords against the decision of the Court of Appeal delivered on 20 May 1993. The Court of Appeal had dismissed his appeal against his conviction for manslaughter on 26 January 1990 at the Central Criminal Court before Alliott J and a jury. He had been sentenced to 6 months' imprisonment suspended for 12 months. The details of the case were:

The original conviction of Dr Adamako arose out of the conduct of an eye operation carried out at the

Mayday Hospital, Croydon on 4 January 1987. The appellant was, during the latter part of that operation, the anaesthetist in charge of the patient. The operation was carried out by two surgeons supported by a team of five nurses and a theatre sister. Anaesthesia commenced at about 9.45 am. The patient was paralysed by injection of a drug and an endotracheal tube was inserted to enable the patient to breathe by mechanical means. At the start of the operation the anaesthetist was Dr Said, a registrar. An operating department assistant was also present to help him. At about 10.30 am there was a changeover of anaesthetists. The appellant was called to attend and take Dr Said's place following which both Dr Said and his assistant departed to deal with another operation elsewhere in the hospital. Another assistant was called to attend but did not arrive until later.

At approximately 11.05 am a disconnection occurred at the endotracheal tube connection. The supply of oxygen to the patient ceased and this led to cardiac arrest at 11.14 am. During this period the appellant failed to notice or remedy the disconnection. The appellant first became aware that something was amiss when an alarm sounded on the Dinamap machine, which monitors the patient's blood pressure. From the evidence it appears that some 4 minutes would have elapsed between the disconnection and the sounding of this alarm. When this alarm sounded the appellant responded in various ways by checking the equipment and by administering atropine to raise the patient's pulse. But at no stage before the cardiac arrest did he check the integrity of the endotracheal tube connection. The disconnection itself was not discovered until after resuscitation measures had been commenced.

At his trial it was conceded on behalf of the defendant that he had been negligent and medical evidence, called by the Crown indicated that the defendant had shown a gross dereliction of care. The judge directed the jury that the test to be applied was whether the defendant had been guilty of gross negligence. The defendant was convicted. He appealed to the Court of Appeal on the grounds that the judge had wrongly directed the jury by applying the test of gross negligence for manslaughter. The Court of Appeal, applying the test that the ingredients of involuntary manslaughter by breach of duty which needed to be proved by the Crown were (1) the existence of the duty, (2) a breach of the duty causing death and (3) gross negligence which the jury considered justified a criminal conviction, and dismissed the appeal on the ground that the jury had been directed according to the proper test and the evidence justified a verdict of guilty. The defendant appealed to the House of Lords who upheld the conviction. His negligence was deemed so wicked that it was criminal

CASE 18 – DP was a 92 year old lady, who lived reasonably independently alone at home. She walked with a stick but was able to manage the multiple stairs in her home. There was a medical background of ischaemic heart disease and atrial fibrillation, for which she was taking regular Warfarin. One evening at approximately 09.30 pm, she fell down the main flight of stairs at home, injuring her back and chest. An ambulance was called and she was taken to the local A&E department. 5 hours later, she was seen and examined by a junior doctor, Y, whose handwritten record noted that she was on Warfarin. Blood tests taken were essentially normal and her INR was 2.1, indicating satisfactory Warfarin control. X-rays were taken but the obvious multiple rib fractures, small apical pneumothorax and surgical emphysema in the right lateral lower chest wall were missed. 11 hours after the fall she was discharged home still on Warfarin with a course of antibiotics and Diclofenac. No-one appraised her domestic situation.

The GP visited the next day and the Diclofenac and Warfarin were stopped. DP failed to improve at home and although the fractured ribs were eventually identified DP refused hospitalisation. 6 days later she entered an intermediate care facility but further deterioration over another 5 days precipitated her hospital admission. A right-sided pneumothorax was discovered and treated by chest drain insertion. There was transient improvement but unfortunately, she developed respiratory distress due to pneumonia, which failed to respond to some 7 days of antibiotics. She died 4 weeks after the fall. Following post mortem examination, the cause of death was given as:

1a) Chest injuries

1b) Domestic Fall

2) Ischaemic Heart Disease

Various statements and the internal hospital review established the following:

i) That over the period of A&E assessment the hospital was extremely busy and the staff were under pressure

ii) Dr Y was inexperienced and had not been pro-actively supported. Dr Y missed the presence of the fractured ribs and not only failed to stop the Warfarin in light of the significant trauma but also prescribed Diclofenac. This medication is relatively contraindicated on the basis of the patient's age and certainly contraindicated on the basis of co-prescription of Warfarin

iii) Her discharge home from A&E was inappropriate on the grounds that the domestic situation was not appraised; there were many steps to access not only her front door, but also her bedroom and no thought was given to supplying her with physiotherapy or occupational therapy, or regular assessment

In my opinion, there were a number of failures in DP's management.

- The obvious fractured ribs were missed. Osteoporosis is almost universal in elderly ladies with the result that fractures are very likely from even trivial falls and especially from a fall down a flight of stairs. As a "general rule of thumb" any elderly lady who has fallen and who complains of pain should be presumed to have sustained a fracture unless proved otherwise. Bleeding occurs around fractures and soft tissue trauma

- The Warfarin was continued. (Warfarin is an anticoagulant frequently given in atrial fibrillation to reduce the risk of stroke. In atrial fibrillation the two atrial chambers of the heart "quiver" rather than beat and small blood clots can form in the relatively stagnant blood therein. If clots pass to the brain a stroke arises. The effects of Warfarin are assessed by a simple INR blood test). Antibiotics and Diclofenac upset warfarin control leading to an enhanced tendency to bleed. This can be reversed traditionally using Vitamin K or by using newer prothrombin complex concentrates such as Octaplex. Reversal is however not instant. If the effects are reversed re-anticoagulation with Warfarin thereafter becomes problematic for up to a few weeks and the risk of stroke rises. Unless there are pressing reasons to reverse Warfarin it is usually best practice to omit the Warfarin for a few days and to allow the anticoagulation to naturally reverse. Thereafter, and if appropriate, Warfarin can be much more easily and effectively re-introduced

- Diclofenac was inappropriately prescribed in conjunction with both Warfarin and her age

- She was discharged home, without any thought for her aftercare

- She ought to have been admitted for a full appraisal and observation and mobilisation

These, in my opinion, were substantial and gross failures on the part of Dr Y which led to and contributed to DP's death. There was a clear and direct causal connection between those failures and her death.

In fact it turned out that it was not all the fault of Dr Y who had been unsupported and unsupervised. There were also serial failures on the part of others. Corporate manslaughter was considered but rejected – as that requires the negligence of a single "directing mind", lesser failings of multiple employees cannot be aggregated together to form the basis for such charges.

CASE 19 – JS was a reasonably fit lady of 84 who sustained fractured ribs and sternum from her seat belt when the car in which she was a passenger had a minor collision. She was admitted to hospital for observation but deteriorated suddenly after two days. She was increasingly short of breath and her blood oxygen saturation levels were deteriorating despite her receipt of escalating and maximal bedside oxygen. At midnight the decision was taken to transfer her to ITU for assisted breathing. This involved a journey of 150 yards through the hospital and a 3 floor lift transfer in the company of two porters and a staff nurse. No portable oxygen was provided and she died in transit. In due course the nurse was charged with gross negligence manslaughter but when questioned made a "no comment" interview and gave no explanation.

When I looked at this case there seemed to be only 2 possibilities, either of which would have satisfied the courts:

1) That the nurse had an indifference to the obvious risk

2) Or that the nurse had foresight of the obvious risk and recklessly went ahead

This case dragged on for two years, much to the discomfort of the nurse before matters were clarified by the statement of one of the porters. He had diligently tried to source portable oxygen to no avail – all cylinders were in use elsewhere. The staff nurse had been faced with a deteriorating patient needing urgent transfer and had made the tough decision to go ahead as the lesser of two evils. Charges were dropped. Had she explained matters early on she would have saved herself much worry!

<u>CASE 20-</u> VM was a man of 75 years recovering in hospital after a major stroke 4 months earlier. He had a urinary catheter in situ and was due for discharge home. {A catheter is inserted into the bladder via the urethra. The male urethra is some 8 inches long, a female urethra is only up to 1.5 inches long. There are male and female catheters with the male catheter being twice as long as the female version. They are anchored in the bladder by inflating a retaining balloon with water}. On the eve of discharge the catheter was removed and there were two

unsuccessful attempts, by nursing staff, to change his catheter. The catheter was left out. At 9 am a reluctant and inexperienced junior doctor, B, was asked to catheterise VM urgently before the ambulance due to take him home appeared. He was given no nursing support for this task and no trolley was laid up for him. Acting alone the doctor selected a female catheter and proceeded. The catheter was inserted more than once, the balloon inflated more than once and significant and inappropriate force was used. There was significant bleeding resulting from damage to the urethra when the balloon was blown up. 3 further but futile catheterisation attempts were rushed to try to remedy the situation quickly before the ambulance arrived. His discharge was prioritised above his medical needs. More trauma resulted and he vomited, choked and rapidly developed an aspiration pneumonia. He deteriorated rapidly and died 12 hours later following a cardiac arrest. Police arrested and questioned "B". However all the elements necessary for a charge of gross negligence manslaughter were deemed to be lacking (catheterisation – even a botched one does not carry a foreseeable risk of death). VM had consented to the catheterisation which ruled out a charge of unlawful act manslaughter. Corporate manslaughter was considered but rejected. There was no individual who could have been considered "the directing mind". Whilst there were multiple minor failings of employees, lesser failures of multiple employees could not be aggregated together (at that time – though the scope for criminal liability was widened in 2008) to support that charge. "B" was not charged with any criminal offence. The coroner issued a narrative verdict. He observed that in the previous 2 years, The National Patient Safety Agency had identified that there had been 114 instances of female catheters being inserted into males. Using Rule 43 he informed those in authority so that they could take action. This resulted in female catheters being withdrawn from general wards in the NHS, though they remain available on Urology wards.

Corporate Manslaughter

The death of Ivy Atkin in Nottingham during November 2012 resulted in the nursing home director, Yousaf Khan, becoming the first person in England to be convicted of corporate manslaughter in a care home. The combination of expert evidence from myself and the pathologist coupled with statements from various members of staff was so compelling that he elected to plead guilty to the offence when he attended court in 2015. He accepted that "the buck stopped with him" and that he was "the directing mind."

Ivy Atkin was an 86 year old lady with a background of advanced dementia and concomitant lack of mental capacity. She was admitted to hospital from home on 19/08/12 and transferred to Autumn Grange Residential Home on 18/09/12. On 02/11/12 the district nursing service received a fax referral which alerted them to the presence of a Grade 4 sacral pressure sore. When seen, she was seated in a wheelchair directly on a metal bar, with no cushion, no footrest and no dressing on the sacral sore. She slept on a normal divan bed and normal mattress which had creased sheets and waterproof protection. Both her clothes and bedding were soaked and she was thin and thirsty. Her care plan was missing. This prompted an immediate Care Quality Commission Inspection which found multiple examples of negligent care involving other residents. (Most of the records from Autumn Grange had disappeared by the time the police investigation commenced). The home was closed and 28 residents immediately removed. Ivy was transferred to another Home on 04/11/12 but despite on-going treatment of her pressure sore, which included tissue viability and dietician input, she deteriorated and died on 22/11/12. Following post mortem examination, the cause of death was given as:

1a) Right Lower Lobe Pneumonia

1b) Debility and low body mass index

2) Dementia

The Home Office Pathologist noted the weight loss and pressure sore, and considered that there was an apparent cause and effect between her care at Autumn Grange, her debility and her death. Her historic weights in July and November 2011 were 6 stones 7lb (42Kg) with the BMI of 18.61 suggesting she was underweight. On 15/09/12 she was recorded as just under 6 stones at 36.45 Kg and at death her BMI was calculated as 10.7. If all weights were accurate, she had lost some 10Kg (1.5 stones) of live weight in the last 10 weeks of her life. This amounted to the loss of a quarter of her body weight. She had been in Autumn Grange for 46 of those 70 days. The statement of one of the carers indicated that residents were rarely helped to eat and that records of food and fluid intake were not only inaccurate but had been completed in advance. Ivy was not on the list of those who needed to be weighed.

When I reviewed the records, I noted the following:

i) From 22/08/12, whilst she was in hospital, the ward nursing staff paid particular attention to her pressure area care. Although her risk was deemed to be mild there was evidence of daily skin assessment until her discharge. She was re-positioned 3-4 hourly, and provided with a foam mattress and foam cushion for sitting out of bed. There was no evidence of any pressure damage when she was discharged and she was able to take food and drink but she was incontinent of urine.

ii) Her GP saw her on 01/10/12 at Autumn Grange for watery diarrhoea. A rectal examination was done and there was no mention of any pressure sore damage. I would have expected, that had there been, it would have been noticed and recorded. She was given Metronidazole for suspected Clostridium difficile diarrhoea. She was next seen by her GP on 23/10/12 because she felt "buggered." She was described as sitting in a comfy chair, was uncooperative and as a result no physical examination was performed. Blood tests were ordered but the patient refused to have them. They were eventually done on or about the 30/10/12. The CRP had risen to 168 and the albumin was low at 20 (these results suggested a significant infection) though her Urea of 6.6 excluded dehydration.

iii) The handover diary from the home had an entry dated 28/10/12 (a Sunday) "*to morning staff on Monday please call D/N for Ivy as she got sore on her bottom*" The daily reporting sheets for the next 5 days recorded her as sitting/resting in the lounge by day. I observed that typically, in a lounge, she would have been sitting upright or semi-upright in in a chair. Her urinary incontinence and diarrhoea were persisting.

iv) I also observed that she would have been particularly susceptible to pressure sores due to various intrinsic factors. These included her immobility, incontinence, underweight status and anaemia which had been recognised and addressed during her hospitalisation. Her risk was enhanced by the onset of watery diarrhoea in early October 2012 and further enhanced from the 23/10/12. She was "buggered", had been uncooperative with offered care and had remained seated for long periods in the lounge with no evidence of any pressure relief.

v) I again observed that Ivy Atkin had evidence of a serious grade 4 pressure sore from 02/11/12 which in all probability was not present on 01/10/12 when her GP performed a rectal examination. It was first noted on 28/10/12. The blood tests of 30/10/12 were consistent with established serious infection which, in the absence of other identified cause, strongly pointed to the source of infection being the presence of established necrosis from the sacral sore. Simply because of her extreme thinness and moisture from incontinence the skin had broken by that point, revealing the damage.

vi) I gave my opinion that the sore developed from the combination of pressure to the sacrum and skin maceration from sitting/lying in moisture such that it was established and infected by 30/10/12. All this stemmed from her reduced mobility and heightened risk after the 23/10/12 which had been wholly and negligently unrecognised and not addressed. Even when the sore was recognised to be present, district nurse referral was not actioned and she remained without any pressure relief whatsoever. She was left sitting for long periods and no care was given to prevent further maceration/infection from her incontinence. Both superficial and deep damage occurred to the sacral area in the last week of October 2012 from wanton and reckless neglect of the most basic principles of pressure area care.

vii) I also gave the opinion that much if not all of her weight loss would have also occurred at Autumn Grange because staff were not monitoring the situation, or feeding the residents. The records were such that poor intake could not be discerned or addressed. The pressure sore especially (attributable to the clear neglect at Autumn Grange) compounded by weight loss would have seriously stepped her down physically, sapped her strength and reduced her resistance to contracting the lethal pneumonia which was the cause of death. By the time she was transferred on 04/11/12 her decline would have been profound such that matters had passed the "point of no return" and her fate was sealed. It was therefore my opinion that there was a causal link between the neglect at Autumn Grange and her death.

viii) The standard of record keeping was also very poor and negligent. They would not have been fit for the purpose of assisting any doctor trying to glean basic information upon which to guide treatment and management. Whether they had been falsified in any way was a matter for the courts not experts to determine. If falsified they could easily have misguided their own staff, visiting professionals from a range of disciplines as well as doctors. Professionals could easily have been beguiled into a false sense of security and given either inadequate or wrong treatment. Falsification of contemporaneous records is serious neglect of a vulnerable adult who cannot give the essential basic information to guide their treatment.

The Bizarre

CASE 21 – JM was an exceptionally fit 94 year old lady, who lived fully independently alone at home. She was born in Donegal and had been in the UK since 1950. She regularly walked miles and did all her gardening, taking pride in her roses on which she regularly spread horse manure. One day, whilst gardening, her leg received a small wound from a rose thorn which she dressed. It slowly worsened. The district nurse attended and asked the GP about giving her a "tetanus jab". Normally tetanus is given at A&E departments, not by the GP. However to spare her inconvenience the GP gave her the "jab" at home. A week or so later she presented at A&E with bizarre symptoms thought initially to be due to a mini stroke. She had a succession of muscular spasms which perplexed the doctors. One violent spasm was witnessed by a young Sri Lankan doctor on observational attachment in the hope of securing a post in the NHS. He alerted her treating physicians to his belief that it was tetanus – unlike UK doctors he had actually seen cases back home. Books were frantically consulted and the diagnosis was correct. She spent 3 months in ITU, followed by 6 months on a rehab unit before returning home in a state of dependency. She successfully sued the GP for negligence – it was settled out of court for a surprisingly large sum reflecting considerable care costs. The GP had given the wrong "jab" because he was unfamiliar with what to do, had never seen anyone unimmunised and had not checked her immunisation status – ignorance was no defence

Annually there are less than 10 recorded cases of tetanus in England and Wales.

Tetanus is caused by the bacteria Clostridium tetani which can survive as spores for a long time outside the body, and are commonly found in soil and manure. If they enter the body through a wound, they multiply quickly and release a toxin that affects the nerves. Symptoms of tetanus usually develop within 4 to 21 days after infection and include stiffness in the jaw muscles (lockjaw), painful muscle spasms which can make swallowing and breathing difficult, a high temperature and fast heart rate. Left untreated, the symptoms worsen over hours and days. Life-threatening suffocation or a cardiac arrest can occur.

The standard "tetanus jab" confers active immunity which takes days/weeks to develop but is long lasting—even lifelong. It does not treat tetanus and does not protect against tetanus for some weeks.

Treatment is by way of human tetanus immunoglobulin which confers passive immunity giving immediate, but short-lived protection—several weeks to 3 or 4 months at most.

In the event of suspected tetanus in someone who has never been immunised, both need to be given.

JM had never received immunisation. Most UK citizens have received full active immunity from childhood immunisation programs, attendance at A&E with minor injury or whilst in the military. Some very elderly females are almost the only people born in the British Isles to be unprotected against tetanus.

CASE 22 – On the night of 17/08/08 at Clayton Manor Care Home in Congleton a fire broke out in the room occupied by an elderly totally dependent resident Mary Bennett. She was found to have black marks on the soles of her feet and died. The soft furnishings in the room had ignited. These were resistant to flame and the fire investigators were fairly certain that this was arson. They would only have ignited if a naked flame had been deliberately applied for some minutes. 7 members of staff were on duty. A police investigation was launched which uncovered evidence of burning to curtains in the room of another equally dependent resident Eve Bain who was also discovered to have dark marks under her toes. I was asked to give an opinion as to their nature and whether they were natural phenomena or possibly related to the main enquiry.

My examination revealed a frail elderly lady, confined to bed with dementia. The toes of her right foot were clawed. In the creases of the 2nd, 3rd and 4th toes, on the under surface, there were small raised dark brown patches, each approximately 1mm in diameter. The skin integrity was not breached and these areas began to easily flake off with gentle pressure.

My opinion was that those areas were entirely natural and non-suspicious phenomena. Specifically, they were the result of accumulation of patches of dead skin and possibly some dirt, which had not naturally been shed, owing to their location in the creases of the toes.

After initial interviews and investigation into care home workers' backgrounds, witnesses were asked for their consent to allow police to look at their medical records. It was this that helped lead detectives to Mary Bennett's murderer, a carer by name of Bowyer. His records revealed that he had started a fire at his grandmother's house in 1998. He had admitted to his grandma that he started the fire and his grandmother then took him to get medical help. He saw a psychiatrist and was assessed, but was found to have no mental health issues.

This knowledge prompted his arrest on 15/09/08. He made full admissions to starting the fire. He said he had done it with the intention of taking his own life and said he didn't want to die alone and that he wanted to die at work with people around him. He had tried to start a fire in Eve Bain’s room earlier that evening.

Chapter Eight

Diabetes, Insulin, Hypoglycaemia, Murder and Incompetence

In the 1970's and 1980's serious complications from diabetes were much more common than now and diabetic ketoacidosis occurred sufficiently frequently for most house physicians to have managed at least a couple of cases during their six months of General Medicine. The management of diabetes has improved due to a combination of better patient education and supervision by specialist teams consisting of diabetes specialist nurses led by consultants. The incidence and severity of diabetic ketoacidosis has fallen and any cases occurring are normally treated by the hospital's diabetes team rather than the on-call physicians. Whilst this has generally been excellent for patient care, non-specialist physicians now have less experience and acute complications can be poorly recognised and badly managed. Whilst I profess no special expertise in diabetes, I have on a number of occasions been asked to review cases and provide a preliminary medico-legal screening opinion from the perspective of a generalist. On occasions diabetic emergencies have been very badly managed and some generalist doctors have chosen to abrogate all responsibility by leaving matters to the specialist nurses. Of all the common conditions seen in hospitals it is my experience that Diabetes Mellitus can be one of the worst managed.

CASE 23 – I H was a 61 year old man, with a background of serious comorbidities, including heart failure, a permanent pacemaker, non-Hodgkin's lymphoma and previous obesity. He had been a type 2 diabetic since 1999 and had been receiving insulin up until around June 2013. According to the evidence of his daughter, he was not taking insulin in September 2013 but was managing his diabetes with diet alone. For a couple of months prior to September 2013, Mr H started to suffer from falls, which were becoming more frequent. He was admitted to hospital on the 11/09/13. Insulin was recommenced during this hospital stay and he then suffered from repeated hypoglycaemic attacks (hypo's), which resulted in his insulin being reduced slightly. He significantly deteriorated on the 19/09/13, culminating in a cardiac arrest in the early hours of the morning of the 20/09/13. At the time of his cardiac arrest, his blood sugar was found to be low at 2 mmol/l.

It was alleged that poor hospital care and management of his diabetes led to his death and I was asked to prepare a report on the issues of breach of duty and causation. To assist me, I was provided with a bundle, approximating to 700 sheets of paginated records. With reference to the pagination, I particularly highlighted from the records the following:

i. Page 7 from November 2012 summarised his significant previous medical history. Page 172 from the 06/06/13, was the note of the diabetes nurse, prior to his discharge in June. I particularly noted the comment *"No further hypos since insulin reduced at last visit, blood glucose levels 5-11 mmol/l currently, no change to insulin dose today"*

ii. Page 69 for the 11/09/13 recorded his initial assessment on arrival in the A&E department. I noted that his blood glucose was recorded at 14.4

iii. His medical assessment, contained on page 73, recorded that he was a type 2 diabetic, on insulin and that there was a history of recent weight loss over the last 6 weeks. The record referred to a weight of 95kg in 2011. Coronary bypass graft, pacemaker in situ and severe left ventricular dysfunction were all noted. Page 79 recorded the differential diagnosis as syncope due to arrhythmia and cause of weight loss. A more detailed medical assessment, contained on page 81, recorded the impression of *"Off legs"* and *"Does not appear to be syncope"*

iv. Page 83 contained the post-take ward round notes, querying the cause for his admission being arrhythmia. He was started on Bisoprolol 1.25mg daily which as evidenced by page 545 was given daily from 13/09/13. (**Comment-** Beta blockers can mask the early warning signs and symptoms of hypoglycaemia, he had not previously been on beta blockers)

v. Page 174, from the 12/09/13, recorded that medicines and insulin were prescribed. Pages 550-551 provided the detail (including the reducing insulin dosage and administration over the ensuing days). His BM was recorded as 11.4 mmol/l. He was seen by a diabetes specialist nurse on the 13/09/13, whose entry was recorded on page 177. "*Denies hypo's at home, BG runs 5-9, aware of DVLA guidance and carried glucose tablets in the car but never needed*" I also noted that his diabetes was managed by his GP. (**Comment-** Contrary to the statement of his daughter it seemed to be assumed that he had been taking insulin at home). It was noted that diet and fluids were being tolerated in good amounts, his BMs (blood sugar levels as assessed by a commercial bedside test) were monitored and insulin given as prescribed. As evidenced by page 184, he was reviewed again by the same diabetes specialist nurse on the 16/09/13, who noted hypoglycaemic attacks over the previous weekend, the details of which were on page 549. She further noted that his Humalog had been omitted 4 times and Humulin I twice. She wrote a message on the chart (page 551) to "NOT OMIT INSULIN. Hypos should be treated as per Trust Guidance and insulin continued as prescribed"

vi. Page 549 contained the records of his blood sugars between the 12/09/13 and the 20/09/13. This sheet spoke for itself, in recording significant and frequent episodes of hypoglycaemia. There were some 10 occasions when the blood sugar was between 3 and 4 and an additional 5 occasions when it was below 3. (**Comment** – the more severe episodes occurred after 16/09/13 when the instruction not to omit the insulin was written)

vii. A different diabetes specialist nurse provided input on the 18/09/13 (page 194), noted his reduced food intake and reduced his insulin very slightly

viii. Page 185 contained the note of the specialist dietician on 16/09/13. His weight was now recorded as 69.9kg, with a BMI of 22. His weight from May 2013 was recorded at 78.9kg, with the estimate that he had lost some 11.4% of body weight in 4 months

ix. Page 194 for the 18/09/13, recorded the notes of the heart failure nurse, who noted the background of known heart failure, that he was admitted due to frequent falls and collapses and that there was no leg oedema and no increasing breathlessness. He was recorded as being on high dose diuretics. Pages 196/197 recorded a ward round on the afternoon of the 19/09/13. It noted that his pacemaker check was satisfactory but that the main finding to date was that he had been having hypoglycaemic attacks. He was noted to be experiencing some depression and it was recommended that he start Citalopram and that a psychiatric review would be needed

x. Pages 197 and 198 contained detailed care plan records, by a student nurse written at 20.40 hours on 19/09/13. I particularly highlighted care plan 3, that 'he had had difficulties making himself understood today, mumbling a lot and not answering questions properly'. From care plan 7, that he had been refusing to have a wash, from care plan 11, that he was requiring the assistance of 1 to transfer. The entry then continued and described that he was not able to mobilise independently and he was very unstable on his legs. He had been presenting with 'some very odd behaviour today, really struggling to communicate, as he mumbled and slurred his words and answered my questions with answers that didn't seem to make sense. His BMs had been very unstable today but regularly checked'. Insulin was administered but minimal amounts of diet tolerated. The patient seemed to be avoiding his daughter's calls to his mobile. Medication taken as prescribed. The next entry on page 198 was the record of the cardiac arrest call, at 03.25 hours on the 20/09/13. This recorded his BM as 2.1, resuscitation was commenced for more than 20 minutes but then discontinued in the light of the multiple comorbidities. His death was certified at 03.30 am. Page 199 contained a retrospective nursing entry, which recorded *"Went to check on the bay of patients and found I H slumped and unresponsive. Crash call put CPR commenced BM checked 2 mmol/l, IV access gained, CPR continued and shock not advised until Arrest Team arrived"*

For the benefit of the court, I observed the following:

- Glucose is the basic fuel of the body and brain. The symptoms and signs of hypoglycaemia (roughly levels below 4) include faintness, weakness, palpitation, hunger and anxiety. These are often associated with sweating. The sweating and palpitations are the early warning signs which can be masked by beta blockers. If not recognised and promptly treated hypoglycaemia will worsen. More severe hypoglycaemia (roughly levels below 3) produces a pattern of neurological signs, including confusion, visual disturbances, motor weakness, ataxia and personality changes. The notes made on the 19/09/13 would be entirely consistent with this. Untreated hypoglycaemia can be quickly fatal especially in those with significant comorbidities. Moderately high blood sugar levels, whilst potentially dangerous in the medium to long term do not cause serious issues over days of poor control if there is some monitoring
- I noted that this man had been losing considerable amounts of weight over the previous months, prior to September 2013. As such, his insulin requirements were likely to have been significantly lower than earlier. It is not certain whether he was taking any insulin at home prior to September or actually needed it. I have seen no evidence that anyone specifically asked him. There appeared to be an assumption that he was taking insulin and that it ought to be continued. He then experienced repeated

hypoglycaemic attacks during his 9 days in hospital. His appetite was reducing and although his insulin dosage was reduced slightly, hypoglycaemic attacks still occurred. The authoritative comment of the diabetic specialist nurse not to omit the insulin but to continue it as prescribed was followed. More likely than not, this worsened the frequency of hypoglycaemic attacks, some of which were severe. Standard practice would have been to fully re-appraise the situation including the need for insulin. Whilst this would best be done by a consultant specialising in diabetes his treating doctors ought to have sought telephone advice about reducing his insulin further or even stopping it temporarily pending that full re-appraisal. They should not have just followed the lead of the diabetes specialist nurses in the face of ongoing and worsening hypoglycaemia. The actions of the diabetes specialist nurses, whilst perhaps reasonable initially on the 13/09/13, then became unacceptable. They failed to respond appropriately such that hypoglycaemia became more frequent and at dangerous levels.

Against this background I gave my opinion as follows:

- In my opinion, this man's overall diabetic management was seriously suboptimal and negligent during September 2013. There was a clear breach of duty in failing to re-appraise his insulin requirements. His actual dose taken at home (if any) was not properly ascertained. There was then a slow and poor response to ongoing hypoglycaemia with instructions not to omit the insulin more likely than not making matters worse. There is no clear evidence that the instructions of the diabetes specialist nurse to maintain his insulin as prescribed, had taken into account his reducing weight and appetite. His doctors failed to provide any input into this at all. Despite the clear evidence of serious hypoglycaemia over the previous days, which they noted on the 19/09/13, they did not take action other than to defer to the diabetes specialist nurse. No-one alerted the doctors to his obvious deterioration on the afternoon/evening of 19/09/13. Had they been alerted and provided a competent response his cardiac arrest would most likely not have occurred.

- In my opinion, ongoing hypoglycaemia caused him to be unnecessarily symptomatic and unwell for much of his 9 day hospital stay. It is also my opinion that the hypoglycaemia in evidence at the time of his cardiac arrest was the cause of the arrest and the cause of his death.
- I accept that this man had significant comorbidities, which would have impacted severely on his life expectancy. However, had he received proper monitoring of his insulin need and proper assessment of his insulin requirements, then on the balance of probability, the cardiac arrest sustained in the early hours of the 20/09/13 would not have occurred and he ought to have lived up to a further 2.5 years.

CASE 24 – D R, an 84 year old lady, died from hyperglycaemic hyperosmotic coma in hospital, at 04.20 hours on the 27/09/08. Many professionals were involved in her care over the preceding 9 days prior to her hospital admission. The police initiated an investigation and I was asked to assist them, by providing a report giving opinions on the roles/actions of each person involved and whether each or any person breached their duty of care, and if so, whether this amounted to gross negligence. I was also asked to give an opinion as to whether any breach of care caused her death.

D R had a background of dense stroke and a supra-pubic catheter making her prone to urinary tract infections. She was also known to be a diabetic, managed on diet alone. She had been living at home, supported by social services and family. Throughout the summer of 2008, social services were increasingly concerned about her domestic situation and following a case conference, held on the 18/09/08, social worker S B arranged her admission to a nursing home on the 20/09/08. It later became apparent that the nursing home was never told that D R was a diabetic.

Prior to this, at 8.00pm on the 18/09/08, D R had been visited by Dr L (duty GP), who noted the presence of a urinary tract infection and that her blood sugar was elevated.

Despite treatment with antibiotics, D R became unwell and confused in the nursing home, from the 23/09/09. Her blood sugar was checked and found to be elevated on the evening of the 26/09/08, which prompted a call to the out of hours deputising service. A Dr Q had a triage conversation with the nurse and was told that her blood sugar was above 33.3 on the glucometer. He agreed to attend and saw her at 9.54pm, noting that she had been taking Amoxicillin but had not taken any antibiotic medication that day. He instructed the nursing staff to give D R 500mg of Amoxicillin that night and commence Metformin therapy. He observed her to be having rigors and not to be responsive.

On the 27/09/08, at 31 minutes past midnight, the nurse called the out of hours service for further advice and this call was triaged by a Dr M, who arranged for a paramedic to be dispatched.

The paramedic noted a reduced Glasgow Coma Scale at 11, that she smelled acidotic, her respiratory rate was 55 and her pulse weak. He confirmed that the nursing home staff were unaware that the patient was diabetic. A drip was inserted, normal saline given and she was admitted to hospital. Despite treatment she was pronounced dead at 4.20am some two hours after arrival in hospital.

The hospital records, post mortem and statements of the doctors left no doubt that the cause of death was due to the metabolic complications of a raised blood sugar, in the presence of inadequately treated diabetes mellitus. Specifically, the biochemical picture was a mixed one, with features of hyperglycaemic hyperosmotic coma, together with features of ketoacidosis. On arrival she had a low blood pressure, a fast pulse, and was peripherally shut down and unresponsive. In effect, she was moribund and it was no surprise that despite medical intervention, she died within 2 hours of arrival at hospital.

I observed and explained to the courts that hyperglycaemic hyperosmotic coma (HHC), previously known as hyperglycaemic non-ketotic coma (HONK), is not a common complication of diabetes but tends to occur more in the elderly with deficient renal and cerebral circulations. The diabetes is often mild and the onset of HHC is often slow and insidious over a week or so. The blood sugar rises and causes the excessive passage of urine, which leads to dehydration and further decreased kidney and brain perfusion. This in turn exacerbates the high blood sugar. Decreased cerebral perfusion decreases fluid intake, which aggravates the dehydration. In effect, a vicious circle occurs, which can, if not identified and promptly treated, lead to coma, acute renal shutdown, acidosis and death. The nursing home records vividly illustrated the development of this vicious circle as follows:-

i) The entry of the 21/09/08 indicates that D R had a fairly quiet previous night, that she was cooperative and able to communicate her thoughts. Significant swallowing difficulties were observed whilst she was taking her medication

ii) The entry for 2.00pm on the 21/09/09 indicates that she appeared comfortable and enjoyed watching TV

iii) The entry of the 22/09/08 (8.30pm) indicated that her suprapubic catheter was bypassing during the previous night and that she was wet ++. It was further recorded that she accepted medications and drinks during the night

iv) The entries of the 23/09/08 indicated that she had a quiet evening, accepting medicines and feeds but her suprapubic catheter was still bypassing

v) She was seen by a Dr K on the 25/09/08, who increased her Amoxicillin to 500mg, 3 times daily

vi) The entry for the night of the 25/09/08 indicated that she was awake for most of the night but quiet, her wet bed had to be changed

vii) The entry of the 26/09/08 indicated that her daughter called and was concerned about her mother. There was a gap in the records (perhaps due to a photocopying oversight), with the next entry being on the night of the 27/09/08, recording the events which led to D R's admission

viii) Blood sugar monitoring was commenced at 9.15pm on the 26/09/08, with recordings of 'high' being registered on 8 occasions, between then and 2.00am.

ix) I noted a single sheet of an 'intake and output' chart, which did not commence until 10.00pm on the 26/09/08, which indicates that she declined to take water, other than 10ml but her urine output was recorded as wet ++.

I noted as follows, the evidence provided and the actions of the individuals involved:

From the statement of the social worker S B, I highlighted the following:

i) That her involvement with D R dated from February 2008

ii) That she was aware that D R had had a stroke, was partially paralysed and was totally bedbound

iii) That she visited D R on the afternoon of the 18/09/08, in order to arrange emergency respite care. She found her to be confused and quite unwell and as a result rang the GP surgery and reported her concerns

iv) She was told that Dr L would visit that evening

v) On the morning of the 19/09/08, she telephoned Dr L, establishing the following:

vi) That Dr L was not going to admit her to hospital

vii) That he had prescribed antibiotics for a urinary tract infection

viii) That she was told that D R's blood sugar was up a little

ix) That she met with the manager of the home, telling her of D R's personal and social needs and specifically that she had been seen by the doctor the day before, was on antibiotics and was not well

x) That she ordered a health information form from the surgery – It became apparent later that the surgery only sent a list of medication

xi) S B next visited D R on the 23/09/08 at the nursing home, finding her still to be unwell and confused. When she expressed concern, she was told that her deterioration was due to her infection

xii) She visited again on the 25/09/08 and upon enquiry, was told that D R was no better. She was reassured by being told that her medication had been doubled

xiii) S B had no further input

I noted from the statement of a Dr R that he last saw D R on the 22/08/08, at which time he diagnosed and treated her with antibiotics for a urinary tract infection. At that time, there was no sugar present in the urine.

The statement of Dr L and his contemporaneous computer entry indicated the following:

i) That he neither knew nor had he previously treated Mrs Ryan

ii) That in response to a request from a social worker for a home visit, he arranged to visit her after surgery on the evening of the 18/09/08

iii) He had established from the records that she was housebound with a stroke and had diet controlled diabetes. He also noted her history of urinary tract infections

iv) That when he saw her, she did not appear to be particularly unwell, that she had just eaten her supper and that her carer was present

v) He noted that she had a urinary catheter in situ and considered that she was likely to have had a recurrence of her urinary tract infection. He prescribed Amoxicillin and also noted that her blood sugar was elevated at 17, which whilst elevated, he did not consider serious, given her history of diabetes and that she had just eaten

M T, owner and proprietor of the nursing home, made a statement indicating that she made an initial assessment of D R on the 19/09/08. Both her statement and her handwritten initial assessment form make no mention of diabetes, though the form does mention the previous stroke and the fact that she had a urinary tract infection, for which she was taking antibiotics. This would support her contention that she was not informed of the presence of diabetes.

J R, RMN, the nurse manager at the nursing home completed the nursing documentation upon admission on the 20/09/08, noting the diagnosis of urinary tract infection. Enclosed within the records was a faxed sheet from the Surgery, timed at 14.37 hours, on the 19/09/08, listing D R's medication, none of which would suggest the presence of diabetes. I further noted that D R was described as having a normal diet but had a poor appetite at present but liked to drink. The medication administration record for D R indicated the prescription and administration of Amoxicillin 250mg, 3 times daily, from midday on the 20/09/08, to and including 8.00am on the morning of the 26/09/08. No further Amoxicillin was administered that day, until a stat dose of 500mg was administered at approximately 10.00pm on the 26/09/08. Also given at that time was Metformin 500mg.

Dr K made a statement relating to her involvement on the 25/09/08. From this statement and her contemporary computerised entry of the 25/09/08, I highlight the following:

i) That she was unaware of her diabetic status

ii) That she was aware of her stroke, urinary tract infection and that she was on antibiotics

iii) That she noted that she had a temperature of 38°C

iv) That she considered that she most likely did have a urinary tract infection and planned to double her antibiotic dose of Amoxicillin to 500mg, 3 times daily and for the nursing staff to request a further review if she had not improved in a few days

v) That she noted that D R was engaging in eye contact with her and attempted to cooperate with examination

Dr Q made a statement and from this and his computerised entry, I note his involvement within the out of hours service, subsequent to 21.28 hours, on the 26/09/08. He was informed that D R had been unwell for the last few hours, had a temperature and high blood sugar. He visited her at 21.54 hours, noting that she had had no antibiotics that day. He increased her Amoxicillin to 500mg, 3 times daily and commenced Metformin 500mg once daily. Both were given. He did not think she was acidotic and considered it appropriate for her to remain in the nursing home.

I noted from his statement that in hindsight, he accepted that he should have conducted a further examination and that he should have admitted her to hospital and that he regretted having not done so. His justification was that she was an elderly lady who he did not want to move late at night, unless absolutely necessary.

Dr M's involvement in the out of hours service commenced at 00.37 hours on the 27/09/08 and on the basis of the information communicated, arranged for her to be reviewed by a paramedic, following which, hospitalisation was arranged. He specifically noted that the nursing home were not aware that she was diagnosed as being diabetic.

I gave my opinions as follows:

1) In my opinion, D R died prematurely, primarily from the consequences of communication errors, by the GP surgery, rather than from individual mistakes.

2) The Surgery failed to communicate to both S B and the staff of the nursing home that she was a diabetic. Had this been known, there is every likelihood that blood sugar monitoring would have been instigated. Had that been done there is the strong probability that her deterioration, due to the urinary tract infection, would have been noted and addressed within a few days of her nursing home admission.

3) The actions of Dr L were quite reasonable under the circumstances.

4) I also noted the lack of communication between the doctors at the Surgery, which led to Dr K visiting this lady, who was ill, without being in full possession of the facts. This would amount to a breach of duty of care. It is my further opinion that at the time of her visit on the 25/09/08, this was, in all probability, the last point at which this D R's life could have been saved, had hospitalisation been arranged. I am not able to say to the criminal standard that her life would have been saved. I considered the actions of Dr K to have been suboptimal in not apprising herself of the full facts, before she went to see this lady (whom she did not know). However, her examination, as recorded, seemed reasonable. Had she known that she was a diabetic and had regular blood sugar monitoring been set in train, more likely than not, her actions would have been different. I would not have expected her to have diagnosed, as a general practitioner,

complicated metabolic syndromes such as HHC, but had she been in possession of the knowledge that the sugar was raised, I would have expected her to have sought more senior advice, which almost certainly would have resulted in hospitalisation, with the likelihood that she would not have died at the time she did.

5) In my opinion, the actions of Dr Q were very substandard, which he himself appears to recognise. However, it is my considered opinion that even had he arranged immediate hospitalisation, the clinical situation had passed the point of salvage and that D R's death was, at that point, inevitable.

6) In summary, my conclusions were:

i) The staff of the GP surgery were collectively negligent in both their internal and external communications but this, in my opinion, fell short of gross negligence.

ii) Dr K was negligent, but not grossly negligent, in failing to prepare herself adequately prior to visiting D R on the 25/09/08. Specifically, she failed to establish her previous health status. The consequences of this were that the seriousness of D R's condition was missed leading to a possible avoidable death.

iii) Dr Q was negligent in not organising hospitalisation when he saw D R on the 26/09/08. The actions he took were inadequate and it is clear that he failed to appreciate the seriousness of her condition. Whilst his failures were worse than those of Dr K, I considered them to fall just short of gross negligence. The consequences of that negligence were minimal on the basis that by the time he saw D R, she was beyond salvage. Even had his negligence been gross negligence, it would not have caused or hastened her death.

iv) None of the other individuals considered could be considered negligent in the discharge of their duty of care.

CASE 25 – The police launched operation Ocelot when 3 insulin-dependent diabetic patients were admitted to hospital on the same day, from the same care home with high blood sugars. A fourth (diet controlled) diabetic had been admitted to hospital a few days earlier. I was asked to provide a report upon the management of these 4 patients prior to 03/08/11.

Police involvement with this case commenced on the afternoon of Wednesday 03/08/11, when they were contacted by the local hospital as there were concerns regarding 3 patients who had been admitted to hospital that day. All were ill with high blood sugars and all were insulin dependent diabetics, residing at the care home and all admitted to the same ward. E M and E S subsequently died but F T survived. Concerns were later raised over historic issues with another patient, E J, who had been admitted to the hospital on the 26/07/11 and died on the 27/07/11. She was a diabetic but diet controlled, and not on insulin.

I noted the facts that there were no specific concerns regarding the management of medication storage and in particular that the fridge containing the insulin medication appeared to be in good working order, and at the correct temperature. I also noted that the 2nd and 3rd August 2011, were particularly hot and humid days, with maximum temperatures of 26 °C and 29 °C respectively (and the care home itself was even hotter)

I reviewed the records of the individuals as follows:-

E J. From the hospital admission records of the 26/07/11, I noted that she was a very frail 94 year old lady with established dementia, who was normally bedbound. She had previously been discharged from hospital on the 21/07/11, with a similar episode of decreased responsiveness, as precipitated her readmission on the 26/07/11. The diagnosis was that of bilateral pneumonia. Blood tests taken revealed a blood glucose of 5.5 mmol (satisfactory) but her elevated sodium at 157 and urea at 40.8 were consistent with dehydration. Her elevated white cell count at 13.5 and CRP at 72, would be consistent with a severe infection. Despite treatment with fluids and antibiotics, her condition deteriorated, with death occurring on the evening of the 27/07/11.

In my opinion, she was an extremely frail 94 year old lady, on a steepening trajectory of decline and my further opinion was that her death resulted from natural causes, entirely unrelated to her diabetic management. I saw nothing untoward in her management, by either the care home or the hospital. The biochemical evidence was consistent with, but not diagnostic of dehydration and in my opinion, was due to the natural process of terminal decline, rather than indicative of any nursing negligence.

F T This 90 year old man was admitted on the 03/08/11, feeling generally unwell. His blood sugar was low at 4 and he was hypotensive, with a previously poor oral intake. He had a long-term urinary catheter in situ, raising the possibility of a urinary tract infection. He was treated with Augmentin, when a chest x-ray showed patchy infiltration, consistent with an infective process in the lungs. His blood sugars were initially unstable but gradually stabilised, culminating in successful discharge on the 18/08/11. I particularly noted from the blood tests that there was no evidence of dehydration whatsoever, with his bloods on the 03/08/11 showing a sodium of

133 and urea of 5.6 (entirely normal). His CRP on admission was 57, falling to 19 on the 09/08/11, being consistent with resolving infection.

In my opinion, this 90 year old man was admitted to hospital as the result of a chest infection, which transiently upset his diabetic control. It was my further opinion that there was nothing untoward in his management by either the care home or the hospital and certainly, nothing to suggest any evidence of dehydration.

E M was a very unstable diabetic, requiring a sliding scale for insulin administration. The specific details of this were given on her medication chart, contained within the appendix. I particularly noted that she was also receiving the antidepressant Sertraline, in a dose of 50mg once daily. Her insulin medication was comprised of baseline long acting Lantus insulin, given at the dose of 7 units at breakfast time, with Novo rapid insulin (short acting) being given on a sliding scale, with breakfast, lunch and dinner. I particularly noted the fluctuating and mostly high blood sugars, recorded subsequent to the 27/07/11 and that the sliding scale insulin medication was not being optimally administered. There were lost opportunities when 'best practice' would have suggested that the community diabetes service should have been contacted.

There was a progressive rise in her blood sugar from the afternoon of the 02/08/11, despite the administration of extra insulin and the encouragement to drink water. At 6.00 am on the 03/08/11, she was seen by a doctor for persistently high blood sugars and further insulin was prescribed. She became unresponsive and was admitted to hospital on the 03/08/11.

The hospital records indicated that on her arrival at 10.05 am on the 03/08/11, it was noted that her blood sugar had been persistently elevated for some weeks. Following initial blood tests, the presumptive diagnosis was that of hyperosmolar hyperglycaemic syndrome, for which she was given fluids and insulin.

I also noted that her sodium was 136 mmol, urea 13.4 and white cell count elevated at 16.5. Subsequent analysis of her sodium levels indicated that they remained within the normal range, through to and including the 11/08/11 but the urea and creatinine levels remained high, suggesting a background of underlying chronic renal impairment.

On the basis of a possible lower respiratory tract infection, she was commenced upon antibiotics on the 03/08/11. By 20.00 hours on the 03/08/11, the focus of concern had centred upon her chest, with assisted ventilation in the form of Cpap being prescribed. There was also evidence of multi-organ failure, with a concomitant poor prognosis, which was communicated to the family that same evening.

The records indicate that her diabetic control was improving by the 05/08/11 but she remained chesty and was considered to have a predominantly left sided basal pneumonia. Constipation was noted. Despite ongoing active therapy, she failed to respond and deteriorated with a Care of the Dying Pathway being commenced on the 16/08/11, following which, she died on the 17/08/11. The post mortem examination indicated death from multi-organ failure, associated with acute peritonitis, bilateral pneumonia and congestive cardiac failure, with diabetic ketoacidosis contributing.

In my opinion, this lady was a very unstable diabetic and in retrospect, should have received some expert advice on future management during July. However, it was my further opinion that although sub-optimal, her management within the care home was fit for purpose, until matters rapidly deteriorated during the evening of the 02/08/11. Nonetheless, medical advice was sought and hospitalisation arranged, without undue delay.

Although the blood sugar was very high on hospitalisation, the other biochemical parameters do not suggest any severe dehydration. There was however evidence of chronic renal impairment and her treatment with Sertraline is known to suppress thirst, which can be particularly problematic during a hot spell of weather.

Her admitting clinicians recognised that she had the hyperglycaemic hyperosmolar syndrome, and treated matters appropriately. With the benefit of hindsight, my best interpretation of the events of the 2nd/3rd of August 2011 was that E M was developing the insidious onset of a chest infection, associated with sepsis, which rapidly destabilised her diabetic control. I therefore had no criticism of her management by either the nursing home or the hospital.

E S The general practitioner records revealed the longstanding diagnosis of diabetes and chronic kidney disease stage 3. Her diabetes had been poorly controlled for some time, despite a major review and change of her insulin medication in August 2010. Her diabetes was controlled by baseline long acting insulin in the morning, supplemented by rapid acting insulin given at breakfast, lunch and dinner. She was also receiving Metformin 850mg three times daily, to enhance the susceptibility of the tissues to insulin. I further noted that there were occasional episodes of refusal, particularly so at 17.00

hours on the 30/07/11 and 13.00 hours on the 01/08/11. A general practitioner note for the 24/06/11 indicates that she had been reluctant to take her Metformin as this had a tendency to cause diarrhoea. A further comment for the 07/07/11 indicates that the Metformin could be broken in half, as the patient had difficulty in swallowing the tablet whole. At this point, I noted records of a Glomerular filtration rate (indicators of renal function), recorded over the previous 12 months. The records for August 2010 and February 2011 indicate that the Glomerular filtration rate was over 60 but on the 23/06/11, it had fallen to 36.

I observed that the dose of Metformin, which E S was receiving, was on the high side. At the time the British National Formulary recommended a usual maximum dose of 2 grams daily but the manufacturer's literature suggested up to 3 grams daily. Although rare, Metformin can provoke lactic acidosis and this is most likely to occur in patients with poor renal impairment. As a consequence, NICE guidance recommended that the dose of Metformin should be reviewed if the Glomerular filtration rate falls to less than 45. In fact, her Glomerular filtration rate had fallen significantly over the previous 4 months, by June 2011 and the dosage had yet to be reviewed by the general practitioner. Her blood sugars were fluctuant during July 2011 and became persistently high from the morning of the 02/08/11.

The hospital admission notes for 10.00 am on the 03/08/11, recorded a high blood sugar, low sodium at 124, elevated potassium at 7.4 and urea marginally elevated at 12.4. She was significantly acidotic, with the doctors concluding that lactic acidosis was the key main feature, with ketoacidosis (DKA) being less so, on the basis of only 1+ of ketones. A urinary tract infection was suspected and she was commenced on fluids, insulin and antibiotics. By 4.00 pm, her potassium, sugar and acidosis had all begun to respond biochemically but the patient's condition had failed to improve in general. She continued to deteriorate on the 04/08/11, becoming unresponsive, with decreasing urine output. A Care of the Dying Pathway was commenced at 14.00 hours on the 04/08/11, with death occurring on the morning of the 06/08/11.

In my opinion, this lady's diabetic management had been sub-optimally managed by her general practitioner for some months, and particularly so for the 5 weeks prior to her death, when Metformin therapy was continued at the previous dose, despite her Glomerular filtration rate having been recorded as having fallen significantly over the previous months. Expert advice, ideally, ought to have been sought. It was my further opinion that her deterioration during the latter part of July and early August was the result of her developing lactic acidosis, due to the relatively high dose of Metformin being prescribed in the presence of deteriorating renal function. This was further exacerbated by the development of a coincidental urinary tract infection. However, it was clear from the results in general that this lady was on a general steepening trajectory of decline, for the months prior to her death and whilst review of her medication in June or July 2011 might have prevented her admission on the 03/08/11 from lactic acidosis, it may not have significantly altered her overall prognosis.

There was no evidence of any significant dehydration and in my opinion, there was nothing untoward in her management by either the care home staff or the hospital.

Having reviewed the extensive documentation, my overall conclusion was that there was nothing to concern the police. The hospital admission and subsequent death of E J was entirely due to natural causes.

The admission of the other 3 patients, all in quick succession on the morning of the 03/08/11, was, in my opinion, entirely coincidental and unrelated to either the ambient temperature or the actions of the staff of the nursing home. The admissions of both F T and E M were precipitated by chest infections, which destabilised their already fragile diabetic control. I found nothing untoward in their management by the nursing home staff and only minor criticisms of the management of E M's diabetes.

E S's diabetes was sub-optimally managed. This was within the remit of the General Practice, not the care home. Whilst sub-optimal, in my opinion, the inactions of the general practitioners were a matter of clinical governance and fell short of gross negligence.

CASE 26 – One elderly man with dementia collapsed suddenly on a psycho-geriatric ward at midnight on a Saturday. He had been given an injection of Fragmin, for VTE prophylaxis, an hour or so before. He was revived given IV fluids (dextrose) and later settled with a mug of Horlicks. There was no proper diagnosis and no investigations were done. He remained physically well over the ensuing days. The following Saturday night, again around midnight, the same thing happened – again roughly an hour after receipt of Fragmin. The medical registrar attended. The elderly man was profoundly hypoglycaemic. Further investigations were set in train. Whilst the medical registrar was still on the ward a second patient also on Fragmin collapsed from profound hypoglycaemia. Both had very low blood sugars; neither were diabetics. It was later established that at the time of the low sugars, the insulin levels were high and there were low levels of C-peptide in both patients.

An internal hospital enquiry commenced but when the same thing happened the next weekend to the same patients, the police became involved suspecting attempted murder by use of insulin.

When I looked at this, three things struck me. Firstly there was a strong temporal relationship between the administration of the Fragmin and hypoglycaemia. There was however nothing wrong with the batch of Fragmin. Secondly the same pair of nurses were on duty when the incidents occurred. Both were part-time and neither had good command of the English language. Thirdly the medical evidence, resting heavily on laboratory data, whilst compelling and adequate for clinical management, may not always be sufficiently robust to withstand forensic and legal examination, especially when the whole case depends upon their reliability. Whilst I realised my limitations in providing opinion, I was however able to suggest lines of questioning when the nurses were interviewed under caution.

In actual fact it turned out not to be deliberate assault but negligent incompetence. Both nurses had thought that Fragmin was in fact Humulin Insulin. Matters were dealt with by the hospital and the NMC rather than the criminal justice system. As you will know, C-peptide is produced by the beta cells in the pancreas when proinsulin splits apart and forms one molecule of C-peptide and one molecule of insulin. Low concentrations of C-peptide are seen when insufficient insulin is being produced by the beta cells or when production is suppressed by injected insulin. Diuretics and alcohol can also cause low C-peptide in some cases.

High concentrations of C-peptide within the bloodstream generally indicate high concentrations of endogenous insulin. This may be due to excessive insulin production by the body, a response to high concentrations of blood glucose caused by glucose intake or insulin resistance. High concentrations of C-peptide are seen with insulinomas and may also be seen with hypokalaemia, pregnancy, Cushing's syndrome, and kidney disease. During an oral glucose tolerance test (OGTT), there will often be a temporary increase in C-peptide concentration. Even though they are produced at the same rate, C-peptide and insulin leave the body by different routes. Insulin is processed and eliminated mainly by the liver, while C-peptide degrades and is removed by the kidneys. Since C-peptide remains in the body for much longer than insulin, normally there will be about 5 times as much C-peptide in the bloodstream as insulin. {With deficient liver and or kidney function there may be variably efficient clearing of insulin and C-peptide which makes results of the C-peptide and Insulin assays very difficult to interpret-especially to the criminal standard.}

The police repeatedly observe that insulin is a very dangerous medication which is readily accessible on wards. It has been used frequently as a method of murder by nurses in hospital. The cases of Beverly Allitt in Grantham, Colin Norris in Leeds and Victorino Chua at Stepping Hill Hospital in Stockport are infamous. Another nurse, Kenneth Barlow in Bradford killed his wife at home in 1957 using insulin to make her stuporous and compliant. He put her in the bath and then he gave her more. She sweated abundantly and vomited. Comatose in the tub, she made no effort to save herself as she slid under the water and drowned.

The verdict was murder: It was Britain's, possibly the world's first case of murder in which the aid of insulin was proven. Barlow was sentenced to life imprisonment.

Insulin Murders is the book written by Vincent Marks, a world authority on insulin, and Caroline Richmond, a medical journalist and writer. It deals with the famous cases and ought to be read by those with an interest in forensic medicine or true life crime. The book deals in detail with the case of Colin Bouwer, a New Zealand Professor of Psychiatry, who murdered his wife in January 2000 by injecting her with insulin after weeks of giving her Sulphonylureas, probably hidden in her food. This had set the scene of repeated bouts of hypoglycaemia associated with high Insulin and C-peptide levels. Her doctors had so strongly suspected an Insulinoma that she had undergone a partial pancreatectomy some weeks before her death.

Chapter Nine

Clostridium Difficile, Sloppy Medicine, Exhumation, Ignorance and the GMC

C. difficile There are numerous scholarly articles in the public domain about this condition e.g. *Consultant.* 2013;53(6):389-395 **Authors:** *SALLY ALRABAA, MD, PAMELA R. NOEL, MD, and TODD WILLS, MD University of South Florida College of Medicine*

Clostridium difficile is a spore-forming, gram-positive anaerobic bacillus that produces exotoxins A and B. In 1935, *C. difficile* was isolated during a study of intestinal bacteria in healthy newborn infants. Because of the difficulty in isolating the bacteria, it was originally named *Bacillus difficilis* (difficult bacillus). In the late 1960s, antibiotic-associated diarrhoea was described, and in 1978, *C. difficile* was identified as the causative pathogen in up to 25% of cases. The earliest cases of *C. difficile* infection were attributed largely to previous exposure to clindamycin, but soon after, this infection was also recognised in patients who had received cephalosporin and quinolones. After the turn of the millennium it became increasingly frequent in the NHS with reported cases rising and peaking at 52,988 cases in 2007. (This seemed to coincide with the use of alcohol hand gel to combat MRSA). I developed particular expertise in the management of elderly patients who had contracted Clostridium difficile and who then developed diarrhoea. For 5 months during 2008, I was the 'link' geriatrician to a pilot Infectious Diseases ward, set up to improve on the management of such patients. There were significant improvements throughout the UK during 2008 but nonetheless as late as 2011 some laboratories did not test stool samples for C. difficile routinely unless the test was specifically requested. I came across a number of cases where clinicians had been falsely reassured because stool samples were reported as "negative for pathogens."

In recent years, the number of C. difficile infections has fallen rapidly. There were 14,687 reported cases in England from April 2012 to March 2013. The vast majority of C. difficile cases occur in people who have had antibiotics. Co-prescription of PPI's seems to increase the risk possibly due to reducing the protective effect of gastric acid. Anti-diarrhoeal medications can be deadly. Most cases develop in a healthcare setting, such as a hospital or care home, but can also occur at home without ever going to hospital. Older people are most at risk from infection, especially those who are frail or with medical conditions. People over the age of 65 account for three-quarters of all cases and severe cases of C. difficile infection can be fatal, especially when they occur in people who are already very ill. It tends to be managed by hospital clinicians and relatively few GPs have experience of dealing with it.

C. difficile bacteria spread very easily through spores. Despite this, C. difficile infections can usually be prevented by practising good hygiene in healthcare environments, such as:

- Washing hands regularly. Alcohol hand gel is not effective against C. difficile spores, so the use of soap and water is essential

- Wearing gloves

- Environmental cleaning using products containing bleach, hypochlorite or other sporicidal agents

Standard advice to those visiting someone in hospital with C. difficile, is that the risk of spreading infection can be reduced by hand washing before and after entering the bed space. Those who have used alcohol hand gel perhaps on entry to the ward ought to be reminded to additionally use soap and water.

A very mild C. difficile infection can usually be controlled by withdrawing treatment with the antibiotics causing the infection.

More severe cases can be treated using the following antibiotics:

- vancomycin

- metronidazole

The condition often responds well to treatment, with symptoms improving in two to three days and clearing up completely within 7 to 10 days.

However, relapse is common, occurring in around one in four cases, and requires further treatment. Some people have two or more relapses.

Life-threatening cases may need surgery to remove a damaged section of the bowel. This is needed in less than 1% of cases.

Severe cases of C. difficile infection can be fatal, especially when they occur in people who are already very ill. There has been a perception that cases arise only from negligence and legal claims have expanded.

CASE 27- Mr A was a 75 year old man with a history of multiple sclerosis, left ventricular hypertrophy, cerebral atrophy, essential hypertension and previous carcinoma of the prostate. He was independent but was slowly deteriorating with regard to mobility from his multiple sclerosis. His general practitioner saw him on the 05/02/09. His speech had become more slurred, he was off his feet and complained of right sided chest and loin pain. He was thought to have either a kidney infection or possibly a right sided pneumonia and hospital admission was arranged.

His medication on admission included Aspirin 75mg once daily, Atorvastatin 20mg once daily, Baclofen 10mg tds, Nifedipine M/R 60mg once daily and Lactulose 10ml twice daily. His condition deteriorated, culminating in death 13 days later, with the cause of death being given as:

1a) Pseudo-membranous colitis

1b) Clostridium difficile (hospital acquired)

1c) Antibiotic therapy for pneumonia

I noted from the post mortem report, that the entire length of the large bowel showed features of marked pseudo-membranous colitis, with concomitant dilatation. I also noted focal atheroma of the cerebral arteries, the presence of left ventricular hypertrophy and narrowing of the coronary arteries, up to 85%, due to atheroma. Both lungs were congested and oedematous, with features of chronic bronchitis and emphysema but there was no evidence of pneumonia, embolism or neoplasia.

Painstaking analysis of the medical and nursing records together with the test results revealed initial diagnostic destitution coupled with some fundamental errors of judgement, which in 2009, were below the standard which Mr A could reasonably have expected to have received. The standard of care, which he did receive, would have been acceptable, perhaps 12 months earlier but the recognition and management of C. difficile advanced considerably during 2008. In summary, the fundamental errors, which I identified, were as follows:

i) That there was no clear working diagnosis on admission which stands scrutiny and the evidence for there being a chest infection on admission was very poor (CRP, CXR & WCC normal). Nonetheless he received an (unnecessary) 7 day course of the potent antibiotic combination Amoxicillin and Clarithromycin. The consequences of this were to considerably heighten his risk of subsequent C. difficile development.

ii) Matters were compounded by the distraction, consequent upon the identification of MRSA on 12/02/09. There was no evidence of an MRSA infection, merely contamination. The consequence of this was that when his temperature spiked on the night of 12/02/09 it was assumed to be due to MRSA and Teicoplanin was added – again unnecessarily.

iii) Although loose stools were identified as early as 11/02/09 and a stool sample sent to the laboratory (as well as on the 07/02/09) the policy of the laboratory not to test for the C. difficile toxin routinely led to false reassurance when the report was interpreted as being negative.

iv) His abdominal distension, coupled with the presence of loose stools set against the background of potent antibiotic therapy ought, in 2009, to have led to consideration of the possibility of a C. difficile infection some days earlier than in fact occurred. Had this happened, the likelihood is that his antibiotic therapy would have been reviewed and an appropriate management strategy followed. Instead the first mention of even the possibility of C. difficile was not until the positive result was communicated on 16/02/09.

It was my opinion that the management of this man in respect of his C. difficile fell below the standards expected at the time in question. The consequence of this was that matters progressed over the ensuing days, such that he was beyond salvage when the diagnosis was finally made. The case could not be defended.

To assist with quantum I advised that although life tables would give the future average life expectancy of a male who is approaching the age of 76 years as a further 12 years of life, in Mr A's case, even if we discount the C. difficile, his known pre-existing problems (as per the PM) would have warranted a discount of at least 60% upon the actuarial average, making his survival to the age of 81 unlikely. Even had he survived, it is more likely than not that his trajectory of physical decline would have been steep, with the strong likelihood of concomitant dependency for much, if not all of that 5 year period.

<u>Case 28-</u> Mrs R was originally admitted to hospital on 22/02/10 with a chest infection and was discharged three days later. She was re-admitted with pneumonia on 11/03/10 and developed C. difficile before being discharged on 27/03/10. She deteriorated at home and was re-admitted on 12/04/10 but deteriorated further and

rapidly such that she died on 13/04/10. It was alleged that her discharge from hospital on the 27th March 2010 was wrong and that her treatment was substandard following her re-admission on 12th April 2010. The defence team for the Trust asked my opinion. I highlighted from her medical records, the following:

i) That she had a history of rheumatoid arthritis which had required Methotrexate therapy and joint replacements. She also had a history of aortic valve replacement, pulmonary fibrosis, left lower lobectomy, atrial fibrillation and for years had been short of breath after only 20 yards of exercise. This set the scene for the events of 2010.

ii) On 22/02/10 she had already received two weeks of antibiotics (one week of Amoxicillin and a second week of Clarithromycin). Between 22/02/10 and 24/02/10 she was given Erythromycin and Co-Amoxiclav. These were stopped on 24/02/10 and she was discharged home with no antibiotics on 25/02/10, being described as comfortable at rest and looking well. Upon re-admission on 11/03/10 her regular medication included Lansoprazole. {**Comment-** By virtue of her previous courses of antibiotics and Lansoprazole therapy coupled with mild immunosuppression from Methotrexate she was at high intrinsic risk of acquiring C. difficile infection. {Indeed C. difficile may have been in her bowel prior to admission in March and only have become symptomatic following further antibiotic prescription. The evidence that she acquired it solely or in part from alleged poor hospital hygiene was weak}.

iii) The hospital prepared a retrospective summary of the admission between 11th and 27th of March 2010. There was radiological evidence of right basal consolidation. She had had an episode of haemoptysis.

There was an increased temperature and presence of yellow phlegm. At least one dose of Cefotaxime and Clarithromycin seem to have been given in A&E. By 21/03/10 she had received 11 days of Augmentin and 10 days of Clarythromycin. On the 23/03/10 C. difficile was isolated from her stool at which point these antibiotics were stopped and Metronidazole prescribed. Her Lansoprazole was temporarily stopped. The contemporaneous notes of 27/03/10 clearly indicated that she was apyrexial, fit and well when discharged. There was a formal discharge letter for the admission between the 11/03/10 and the 27/03/10. This letter was dated the 13/04/10 and as such, would have been no use to the GP. It does however confirm that she received intravenous Augmentin and oral Clarithromycin, with the intention to have a 14 day course of Metronidazole. However there was also a shorter discharge summary dated 01/04/10 and stamped as received by the General Practice on 07/04/10. This letter spoke for itself in clearly outlining the onset of diarrhoea due to C. difficile. This information was also recorded on other pages of GP records.

iv) From various records I was able to piece together the actions of the general practitioner. I noted that on the 09/04/10 there was a telephone conversation in which it was recorded that she was still suffering from severe diarrhoea. The GP, Dr B, suspected viral gastroenteritis and issued prescriptions for Dioralyte and Loperamide tablets {**Comment** – this was despite the clear information about the C. difficile stamped as received by the General Practice on 07/04/10}. Her husband went to the surgery to collect Dioralyte and Loperamide tablets. I also noted that on the 12/04/10, there was a further phone call, dealt with by another GP, Dr C, whose records suggested that she was weak, still suffering from diarrhoea and vomiting and had fallen. That precipitated hospital re-admission. I further noted that on the 12/04/10, the surgery received the results of a faeces sample, which clearly stated that no pathogens were isolated. {**Comment** – the authoritative BNF indicates that Loperamide is contraindicated in the presence of antibiotic associated colitis. It may mask symptoms and predispose to colonic dilatation and thus precipitate the onset of sepsis. I also noted the result of the faeces sample and suspect that testing for C.difficile was not specifically requested. In 2010, many laboratories did not test for it routinely, unless specifically asked. I noted from the hospital admission of the 12/04/10 that her deterioration had worsened some 3 days before the 12/04/10, correlating with the prescription of the Loperamide}.

v) I particularly noted that upon re-admission on the 12/04/10 and as evidenced by the high CRP of 313, her white cell count of 11.1 and tender abdomen, she was unwell. The onset of fast atrial fibrillation posed as a cardiac arrest. This was followed by poor urine output, an elevated white cell count of 28.3 and the onset of metabolic acidosis consistent with septic shock.

vi) I noted that although C. difficile was diagnosed early in admission and the correct treatment of Metronidazole and Vancomycin prescribed, oral Vancomycin was not actually given until the 13/04/10. The nursing records confirmed that Vancomycin was unavailable on the ward and not actually given until the 13/04/10. {**Comment** – I noted that the 12/04/10 was a Monday and although it may have been late afternoon before the prescription was written, there is no evidence that anybody tried to source the Vancomycin from either other wards or from the pharmacy. This delay in receiving Vancomycin was unfortunate but may in fact have made little difference to the outcome given how unwell she was}.

My opinions were that by virtue of her previous use of antibiotics, Lansoprazole therapy and mild immunosuppression from her Methotrexate, she was at high intrinsic risk of acquiring C. difficile infection. C. difficile may have been in her bowel, prior to the 11/03/10 and only have become symptomatic following antibiotic prescription. The evidence that she acquired it solely or in part from alleged poor hospital hygiene was weak. She developed diarrhoea, around the 21/03/10, confirmed as C. difficile positive. This was identified and treated with Metronidazole.

There was good evidence that she had significantly improved by the 26/03/10 and on the basis of the evidence that I saw, it appeared entirely reasonable to have allowed her home. Being at home, would have improved the chances of the C. difficile clearing up, remaining in hospital would have enhanced her risk of re-infection.

It was clear to me that the general practitioner was provided with all the important details about her admission in March 2010, prior to 09/04/10 and prior to the discharge letter dated the 13/04/10. My opinion was that Dr B (by suspecting viral gastroenteritis on 09/04/10 and failing to note the C. difficile history and Metronidazole prescription) had not read the information in the GP records when he issued his prescriptions. Mrs R was never seen or examined. Whether his actions amounted to breach of duty was a matter for a General Practice Expert. One issue was that the prescription of Loperamide in the presence of antibiotic associated colitis is contraindicated. A second issue was that C.

difficile is much more likely to be managed by hospital physicians, than GPs. As such I would have expected that a general practitioner confronted by a patient with known C. difficile and on-going diarrhoea despite Metronidazole to have sought hospital advice.

On the matter of the causation of her final decline, it was my opinion that the delay in hospital re-referral coupled with the prescription of Loperamide allowed a likely salvageable situation to progress to a critical and probably unsalvageable situation by 12/04/10. It was my further opinion that the prescription of Loperamide would not only have masked symptoms, but also have made matters worse rather than better. It may have precipitated the deterioration possibly by colonic dilatation, which led to the onset of septic shock.

Following readmission on the 12/04/10, it was my opinion that this lady was extremely ill and given her pre-existing comorbidities, was very unlikely to have survived septic shock, regardless of what therapy was given. It was my opinion that the clinical appraisal of the situation, from very early on that admission, was thorough and thoughtful and that the right forms of treatment were prescribed, supported by active management with fluids etc.

The claimant withdrew the claim against the Trust and went in pursuit of the general practitioner.

When Sloppy Medicine Thwarted a Claim

Case 29- For some months prior to her death in 2002, Mrs T, a lady of 89 years, had been cared for at home by her son, during which time her health was in steady and accelerating decline. Predominant amongst her symptoms was a decline in her swallow, such that she was having difficulty in eating and drinking. This was confirmed by a video fluoroscopy. She was seen by Dr M in clinic on Thursday 16/05/02. Although there is no evidence that she was examined, Dr M arranged for her to be admitted on Friday the 17/05/02 for investigation and consideration as to whether a PEG tube should be inserted. She was admitted to a ward at the hospital during the late afternoon but not examined by any doctor. No chest x-ray or blood tests were performed. She was found dead in bed, having died between 3.15 and 3.50 am on Saturday 18/05/02. Dr M issued a death certificate, as follows:

1a) Aspiration pneumonia due to:

1b) Bulbar palsy

1c) Cerebral vascular disease

1d) Ischaemic heart disease with congestive cardiac failure

Her son was convinced that the care his mother had received from Dr M was so grossly negligent that it resulted in her death from dehydration. His belief was so strong that he pursued matters with great vigour and even arranged a private exhumation of the body in mid-2004 with a post mortem performed by a Home Office pathologist, who, unsurprisingly, was unable to determine the cause of death.

A lengthy inquest was held in July 2007, by the coroner who was assisted by 2 medical experts, who had been appointed by Mr T. The coroner was unable to establish a cause of death and issued a narrative verdict, which indicated that Mrs T was probably dehydrated, to an unknown extent, at her time of death. Having failed to gain support for criminal charges the son attempted to sue Dr M in the civil courts and have him sanctioned by the GMC. When I looked at this case the basic problem was the lack of actual medical facts which eventually thwarted any claim.

I observed that issues regarding facts are matters for the courts, not for experts to determine. There was no evidence of clinical examination, no evidence that any blood tests were performed and no evidence that she had a chest x-ray during the time her health was in decline. Had these tests been done, they would have established the facts and without them, the facts could never be determined. Whether or not pneumonia or dehydration were present, could only be a matter of educated speculation, which left substantial doubt as to their presence or absence.

I made the following points:

i) All the evidence pointed to the fact that her swallowing was deficient, due to neurodysphagia, most likely due to cerebral vascular disease. As such, this would be better described as a pseudo bulbar palsy, rather than a bulbar palsy

ii) Given this lady's rapid trajectory of decline, her life expectancy was unlikely to have exceeded 4 months from her date of death, even had possible dehydration been identified and treated. Insertion of a PEG tube carries a significant mortality rate but even had successful insertion been performed, dehydration been prevented and her quality of life improved the extent of future life may not necessarily have been prolonged

iii) There was strong likelihood that over the weeks prior to her death, she was progressively dehydrating and that this tendency was being exacerbated by her ongoing diuretic therapy

iv) The clinical diagnosis of dehydration without blood tests is extremely difficult in elderly patients

v) The likelihood was that this lady suffered a sudden cardiac death in her sleep, in which case, electrolyte imbalance, coupled with her known ischaemic heart disease, may have been significant. Electrolyte imbalance is often a feature of dehydration but there are other causes

vi) The evidence for aspiration pneumonia/ pneumonitis was weak

vii) There was evidence of poor communication with regard to this patient's management, between the clinic appointment on the 16/05/02 and her death. Specifically, I identified the following deficits:

a) Whilst Dr M may have given instructions to his team verbally regarding the plan of management, this plan was not communicated to the junior doctors covering between 5.00 pm and 9.00 pm and as a consequence, no communication was given to the junior doctor covering at night

b) There was poor evidence that Dr M's management plan was communicated to the nursing staff on days and as a consequence, no management plan was passed to the nursing staff on nights, upon whom it fell to communicate with the doctor covering

c) It was likely that Dr M's plan was originally to admit this lady much earlier during the day on the 17/05/02 and there is evidence that a phone call was made by the Bed Bureau, indicating that a bed was available. Unfortunately the son was out when the phone call was made and as a consequence, Mrs T's admission occurred some hours later than would have otherwise been the case

In retrospect, the following measures could have been taken by Dr M and would have been best practice:

i) Routine blood tests, including haemoglobin and U&Es could have been taken in clinic on the 16/05/02

ii) He could have coordinated better with the ward and indicated to the son that the earlier Mrs T arrived on the ward during the day, the better. Even if a bed had not been available immediately, she could have been seen and assessed by the doctor. As it was, the breakdown in communication, coupled with her late arrival on the ward, conspired to set in train the sequence of events, which led to this lady being unassessed and uninvestigated throughout the 17/05/02.

My opinions were that the cause of death, namely aspiration pneumonia, as described by Dr M, was wrong and my further opinion that the most likely cause of death was a sudden cardiac event. There was a strong likelihood that Mrs T was suffering from a degree of dehydration during the last few days/hours of her life. In the absence of facts, this is educated speculation. Had the fact of dehydration been established and had it not been treated, then the dehydration could well have been a factor in the cause of death. As it was, I did not know whether she was dehydrated or to what extent and on the basis of those known unknowns, I could not attribute her death to dehydration.

The presence of dehydration or not was the crucial issue. This fact should have been identified. Clinical examination probably ought to have been performed but it is unlikely to have been helpful in determining the presence of dehydration or not. This can only be established through basic blood tests, which ideally should have been performed in clinic on Thursday 16/05/02 by Dr M himself, or else performed during the day, of Friday 17/05/02, on admission. It was my opinion that the responsibility for this rested with Dr M, who should either have arranged them himself on the Thursday or else made a robust plan for them to be performed on the Friday. He could and probably should have checked with the ward around 6.00 pm with a simple phone call, to check that she had arrived and to check that the doctors were aware of his plan. This was, after all, Friday and there is little point in admitting a patient late on a Friday as a routine admission, if the plan of action is not communicated. Patients, such as Mrs T, electively admitted can in fact be much more ill than patients who present as 'an emergency'.

My opinion was that in respect of not establishing the facts regarding dehydration, Dr M was negligent, but not grossly negligent. He either should have arranged basic blood tests himself or made robust arrangements for them to be done. As it was, he did neither and the consequence of this, more likely than not, was an otherwise preventable death from a sudden cardiac cause, secondary to a likely treatable dehydration. It was my further opinion that this would probably fulfil the criteria for a successful civil negligence case (though given her poor prognosis and limited life expectancy the quantum would be low) but would be unlikely to succeed in the criminal courts. On the basis of lack of fact, there must be reasonable doubt as to whether dehydration was present and whether the electrolytes were disturbed.

I found no evidence that the actions of others were either negligent or grossly negligent.

Exhumation

'Exhumation' is simply the removal from the ground of the remains of a human being, either in the form of a body or cremated ashes. They are rarely done and tend to be traumatic for the family involved. They can take a long time to arrange and are usually expensive. For these reasons, it is always best to consult with all the relatives before proceeding. Excepting pursuit of evidence for the purposes of the criminal courts, the usual reasons for exhumation are:

- To move a body from the original grave site to a new grave
- To deepen an existing grave for a further burial
- To send them for cremation

A licence from the Ministry of Justice is needed to remove human remains from the ground. If the remains are in consecrated ground then permission must also be obtained from the Diocesan Court. The signatures of any close relatives, the owner of the grave plot and the burial authority are required.

There is no charge for a licence but there may be significant fees charged by the burial authority and whoever carries out the exhumation. Costs include

- Memorial removal costs
- Funeral Director's charges, including the cost of a new coffin or cremated remains casket
- Cemetery fees and charges for exhumation and re-interment by the local authority

There are issues to preserve decency and safety.

Both an Environmental Health and Cemeteries Officer are often present at the exhumation and will supervise the event to ensure that respect for the deceased person is maintained and that public health is protected. The Officer/s will also ensure that:

- The correct grave is opened,
- The exhumation commences as early as possible in the morning to ensure maximum privacy,
- The plot is screened as appropriate for privacy,
- Health and safety of all workers is maintained e.g. protective clothing including masks and gloves, task lights and all other necessary equipment is provided,
- Everyone present shows due respect to the deceased person and to adjoining graves,
- The nameplate on the casket corresponds to that on the licence,
- The new casket has been approved
- All human remains and all the pieces of casket are placed in the new casket,
- The new casket is properly sealed,
- The area of exhumation is properly disinfected, and
- Satisfactory arrangements are in place for the onward transmission of the remains.

If the conditions of the licence cannot be met, or there are public health or decency concerns, the exhumation may not proceed.

Concealing a Body and Preventing a Burial

The rules governing exhumation are matched by ones determining proper disposal of a corpse. The law requires that death must be reported and bodies appropriately disposed of. Periodically, family members choose not to report deaths and continue to live with the deceased for many months whilst the body slowly decomposes. Normally, when discovered, advanced decomposition thwarts the establishment of the cause of death at post-mortem examination. Such cases usually result in prosecution for the offences of concealing a body and preventing a burial. Sometimes prosecution for fraud is added to the charge sheet if the pension of the deceased has been accessed by family members – actual payment of the pension into a bank account cannot be stopped without a death certificate but if it is then withdrawn by someone using a debit card that is usually sufficient to support a charge of fraud.

Mistakes and the GMC

It is well recognised that on most days, many people will make a mistake. These are normally small and inconsequential errors that are never discovered or result in no harm. The art of risk management is to balance proportionately (in a user-friendly practical manner) the potential for human error against the degree of risk. The 'Swiss cheese' model is often quoted with regard to risk management. The holes in a pile of slices of Swiss cheese represent failures in a system's defences that allow a hazard to pass through. A critical incident occurs when all of the holes line up. When doctors make a mistake, a GMC referral can result. "The Fitness to Practise Committee" will usually screen out those of a malicious and unfounded nature. Where standards of care appear to have been low they will often seek expert opinion structured around specific questions. The key issue which they wish to establish is whether standards have fallen seriously below that expected of a doctor of that grade and specialty. I have dealt with many of these cases and include my redacted case report below in its entirety to illustrate the required format and the consequences of ignorance regarding recognised complications of Warfarin therapy:

Case 30 –

MEDICAL REPORT ON: Actions of Dr O

RE: Medical Care on 14/XX/XX

AT THE REQUEST OF:XXXXXX

General Medical Council

350 Euston Road

LONDON

NW1 3JN

1) I am Dr Geoffrey Phillips and I hold the qualifications MBBCh (Bachelor of Medicine and Bachelor of Surgery), and have been a Fellow of the Royal College of Physicians of London since 1993. I held the position of full time consultant geriatrician within the Liverpool Teaching Hospitals between 1982 and May 2011. I was also an honorary lecturer in the University Department of Medicine. Following re-organisation within my main hospital base, I took the opportunity to retire from the NHS, in good standing, and In May 2011 entered full time independent practice.

2) My daily practice involved dealing with the full range of medical illness, which affects the elderly. This included acute medical care, together with rehabilitation and the assessment of disability. I have particular expertise in the assessment of continuing care needs and regularly assess patients, either in their own homes or in nursing homes, at the request of general practitioners.

3) I have been asked to provide an independent report to assist the General Medical Council, in their investigation of a complaint against Dr O who describes himself as a Senior Trust Grade Doctor in elderly care. I have no conflict of interest in this matter. I have set out the essence of the complaint in paragraphs 5 and 6.

4) To assist me, I have been provided with a bundle, containing:-

- Referral letter dated 18th XXXXX (DOC ID: 56xxxxxx)

- Rule 4 comments from Dr O (DOC ID: 56xxxxxx)

- Complainant's response to Dr O's Rule 4 comments (DOC ID: 56xxxxxx)

- Redacted GP records Patient F (DOC ID: 55xxxxxx)

- Redacted GP records Patient F (DOC ID: 56xxxxxx)

- Redacted Hospital records Patient F (DOC ID: 56xxxxxx)

- Redacted Hospital records Patient F (DOC ID: 56xxxxxx)

- Redacted Hospital records Patient F (DOC ID: 56xxxxxx)

• Redacted Hospital records Patient F (DOC ID: 56xxxxxx)

• Redacted Hospital records Patient F (DOC ID: 56xxxxxx)

Background to the Case

5) At the time in question, patient F was an 83 year old inpatient at XXXX Hospital, who had been diagnosed with and treated for a urinary tract infection. She was also receiving Warfarin and was anticoagulated. On the afternoon of the 14th, her daughter-in-law (a GP) visited patient F, whom she noticed to be unwell. She raised her concerns with the nursing staff and later, with the medical team. Dr O was heavily involved with her care, until approximately 10.00 pm that day. Patient F was complaining of abdominal pain and an abdominal mass was palpable. This was originally thought to have been a palpable bladder but eventually a rectus sheath haematoma was diagnosed and treated. Treatment involved cessation of Warfarin therapy and the administration of vitamin K. Her Warfarin was discontinued and during the admission, she was transfused 5 units of blood. She was successfully discharged. I note for completeness that she was readmitted 3 weeks later, with bilateral DVTs and bilateral pulmonary emboli. At this point, anticoagulation was recommenced.

6) It is alleged that Dr O:

i) Failed to take an adequate history and perform an adequate examination

ii) Failed to diagnose a life-threatening emergency

iii) Failed to respond to the concerns expressed by relatives and nurses

iv) Failed to treat an acute abdominal bleed

v) Failed to report a serious condition to his superior consultant

vi) Displayed a patronising and belligerent attitude towards a relative who was trying to impress the seriousness of the situation

vii) Put the patient's life in danger

Specific Issues to Address

7) I have specifically been asked to deal with 13 issues which I shall reproduce in paragraph 20 and answer in paragraph 21.

Review of the Facts as Now Known

8) Whilst it is ultimately the place of the "Fitness to Practise Panel" to determine the facts, the key facts appear to be:

i) That patient F developed a significantly large rectus sheath haematoma

ii) That this was not considered as a potential diagnosis

iii) That further investigations were not arranged until after midnight on the 14th

iv) That the correct diagnosis was not established until after a CT scan, at 04.30 am

Review of the Care of Patient F

9) It is recorded that Dr O saw patient F at 10.20 hours on the 14th, at which time she was medically stable and keen to go home.

10) Dr O saw her again at 12.04 hours on the 14th, after patient F had had an episode of collapse, after using the commode. He recorded that she had had a similar episode earlier in the morning, when mobilising from the toilet. She had become grey and drowsy on both occasions. He noted that she had become hypotensive and that her blood pressure improved subsequently. His examination established that she was maintaining her own airway, breathing with a respiratory rate of 18 and her sats were 97% on air, her blood pressure was 82/44 and heart rate was 64. Her ECG showed no acute changes and his diagnosis was a likely vasovagal/syncope +/- pre-micturition syndrome, possibly secondary to her anti-hypertensives. His plan was for her blood pressure to be checked and if still low, she was to be given intravenous fluid. Her blood pressure was to be checked on both lying and standing and he considered stopping her Amlodipine.

11) A nursing entry, timed at 13.00 hours, recorded her as seeming more settled, although her blood pressure was noted to decrease when she was standing. A urinary output was noted to be low and this was associated with a swollen abdomen. Medical review was requested.

12) A further nursing review occurred at 16.00 hours on the 14th, at which point she appeared grey and was reporting abdominal pain. A Dr R (FY1) attended and performed an abdominal examination, diagnosing constipation and urinary retention. A postural drop in blood pressure was noted and intravenous fluids were commenced.

13) The entry of Dr R timed at 16.20 hours on the 14th, indicates a palpable bladder, she was unable to urinate when placed on the commode and a catheter was inserted.

14) Dr O made a retrospective entry at 17.07 hours on the 14th, recording his conversations with the daughter-in-law. He recorded that the daughter-in-law told him she was concerned about what she saw as a sudden deterioration, specifically, the daughter-in-law was recorded as asking the following questions:

i) Could she have had an MI?

ii) Could she have had a GI bleed?

iii) What is the cause of her abdominal swelling?

iv) Are you going to perform a troponin-T test?

15) Dr O recorded that he had explained that neither an MI nor a gastrointestinal bleed would be his first differential, as there was no evidence to support either. He explained that the distended abdominal mass was arising from the pelvis and was most likely to be a urinary bladder. He also recorded that he mentioned to the daughter-in-law that she was on the ward as a relative, <u>not</u> as a clinician. At this point, I note the presence of a Witness Statement within my bundle, from a Band 5 Dietician, who had been present for part of the conversation between Dr O and the daughter-in-law. No concerns had been raised about his attitude.

16) Dr O reviewed patient F again on the 14th, making a retrospective entry at 9.35 pm. He reconfirmed the examination findings of Dr R earlier and his impression again was that the problem was due to urinary retention, the tense lower abdominal mass he thought was consistent with a distended bladder. Patient F's blood pressure was 148/80 and pulse 73. He noted that there was 100ml in the catheter bag but asked for a bladder washout and change of catheter, in case it was in an incorrect position. He considered performing a

bladder scan, but there was no working bladder scan in the hospital. He considered that if there was no passage of urine after an enema, then the catheter should be changed to one with a larger gauge. If then there was a failure to pass urine, she would need review by the night team and possibly transfer for a suprapubic catheter. He arranged handover to the night team.

17) A different doctor, Doctor K, was asked to review her at 11.50 pm on the 14/02/14, at which point there was a large, mildly tender and asymmetrical suprapubic mass. The catheter was changed and she was reviewed again at 00.50 hours on the 15/02/14. Only a small amount of urine had been obtained. It was now considered to be very unlikely that the mass was a distended bladder. At this point, the Radiological Registrar was contacted.

18) The radiologist performed an ultrasound scan, revealing an empty bladder and then proceeded to a CT scan, which showed the large rectus sheath haematoma, with distention of the abdominal wall. This prompted the cessation of Warfarin treatment, the administration of vitamin K and the commencement of intravenous fluids and cross-matching of blood.

Overall Opinion on the Management of Patient F

19) With the benefit of hindsight, it is clear that patient F was sub-optimally diagnosed and managed, whilst under the care of Dr O. Rectus sheath haematomas are well known to occur in patients on Warfarin but they are relatively rare. Dr O did not consider this within his differential. A reasonably competent clinician, holding the position of a Senior Trust Grade Doctor in elderly care, ought to have realised by 9.35 pm on 14th that the clinical scenario no

longer accorded with his presumptive diagnosis. All the facts were at his disposal. The swelling remained after catheterisation and there was some urine in the bag, the blood pressure had been variably low and there was a history of fainting. This ought to have prompted a full re-appraisal of the situation. This was partly done by his request for a "bladder scan" but thwarted by lack of a working scanner. Nonetheless, his examination findings and overall assessment appeared adequate and had excluded both an MI (heart attack) and GI (intestinal) bleed. He had arranged hand over and further review. Quite frankly there was little other than a rectus sheath haematoma which would fit the findings. Why it was not considered is ultimately for Dr O to explain. My opinion is that it was not considered because quite simply Dr O was unaware of this complication. At his grade he ought to have been. Not to have known of this complication and to have considered it early fell below the standard expected of a reasonably competent Senior Trust Grade Doctor in elderly care. Many elderly patients are in receipt of anticoagulants and a competent Senior Trust Grade Doctor ought to be aware of the complications, be they common or rare. This was his only error. The rest of his actions were competent which is why my opinion is that I do not believe that his care fell **seriously** below the standard of a reasonably competent Senior Trust Grade Doctor in elderly care.

Structured Opinion on the Management of Patient F

20) The questions and my answers are as below:

Questions:

Q1 Whether Dr O obtained an adequate medical history

Q2 Whether Dr O conducted an adequate examination

Q3 Whether Dr O responded adequately and appropriate to patient F's:

i) Presenting conditions

ii) Test results, where applicable

iii) Medical history

Q4 Whether Dr O correctly diagnosed patient F's condition and adequately considered alternative diagnoses in the light of patient F's presenting conditions and symptom history

Q5 Whether Dr O arranged or carried out appropriate tests or further investigations

Q6 Whether Dr O adequately considered the need for any referrals and acted adequately and appropriately in arranging such referrals

Q7 Whether Dr O ensured adequate management and monitoring of patient F's condition

Q8 Whether Dr O communicated adequately and appropriately with patient F and/or other parties and provided appropriate communication, support and advice

Q9 Whether Dr O followed relevant protocols, guidelines or best practice

Q10 Whether Dr O adequately recorded information in patient F's medical records

Q11 Whether the overall standard of care provided by Dr O fell below that expected of a reasonably competent Senior Trust Grade Doctor in elderly care

Q12 Whether the overall standard of care provided by Dr O fell **seriously** below the standard of a reasonably competent Senior Trust Grade Doctor in elderly care

Q13 Whether any other issues are relevant to this case

21) **Answers:**

A1 Yes

A2 Yes

A3 i) Yes he did initially, but failed to reappraise the situation and consider alternatives when the catheter failed to relieve the abdominal swelling.

ii) Regarding test results, he attempted to arrange a bladder scan but was thwarted by the lack of a bladder scanner. In my opinion, an ultrasound scan ought to have been arranged in the Radiology Department earlier than was in fact the case.

iii) Regarding medical history, having excluded a myocardial infarct and GI bleed and then having established that the abdominal mass was not draining following catheter insertion, he ought to have reappraised the whole situation, looking for an alternative likely diagnosis. A rectus sheath haematoma would have been an extremely likely diagnosis, given the fact that she was on anticoagulants. The fact that he did not consider this was highly suggestive of his ignorance about this rare but well-recognised complication of anticoagulants.

A4 No. He failed to adequately diagnose patient F's condition and failed to consider alternative diagnoses in the light of the evolving circumstances.

A5 Partially, in that he was thwarted in arranging a bladder scan, by lack of functioning equipment but at that point, he ought to have arranged an abdominal ultrasound scan.

A6 No. His focus appeared to be on the fact that this was a distended bladder and whilst his actions were appropriate in the event of it having been a distended bladder, they were inadequate given the eventual diagnosis.

A7 Yes. His monitoring and management were reasonable.

A8 Yes. His records and the supporting Witness Statement suggest that his communication was adequate.

A9 Yes. In that he considered that there was a swollen bladder, he followed all the protocols and guidelines, however, had he considered the alternative and indeed in retrospect, the correct diagnosis, the alternative treatment instigated later should have been introduced earlier.

A10 Yes. His record keeping was good.

A11 Yes. In my opinion, the overall standard of care provided by Dr O fell below that expected of a reasonably competent Senior Trust Grade Doctor in elderly care. Many elderly patients are in receipt of anticoagulants and a competent Senior Trust Grade Doctor ought to be aware of the complications, be they common or rare.

A12 In my opinion, Dr O's actions were perfectly reasonable, given his ignorance of the rare complication. Had a bladder scan been working, the diagnosis would have been established much earlier. Nonetheless, he arranged appropriate handover care and seems to have reacted appropriately to the concerns of Dr F. I do not therefore believe that his care fell **seriously** below the standard of a reasonably competent Senior Trust Grade Doctor in elderly care.

A13 I raised and dealt with the main issue relevant to this case, in paragraph 19 above. I would reiterate that the fundamental error here was that Dr O was ignorant of the fact that rectus sheath haematoma are rare but well-recognised complications of anticoagulant therapy. Had he been aware of this simple fact, the diagnosis would almost certainly have been made up to 10 hours earlier.

Conclusion

22) In conclusion, my opinion is that Dr O failed to diagnose a rare but well-recognised complication, out of ignorance. This ignorance fell below the standard of knowledge expected of a reasonably competent Senior Trust Grade Doctor in elderly care. His actions otherwise appeared quite competent. I do not therefore believe that his care fell **seriously** below the standard of a reasonably competent Senior Trust Grade Doctor in elderly care.

My statement of truth is included.

Yours sincerely

DR G PHILLIPS FRCP

Consultant Physician in Geriatric Medicine

Statement of truth

"I understand that my primary duty in written reports and giving evidence is to the Fitness to Practise Panel rather than to the party who engaged me.

(i) I have endeavoured in my report and in my opinion to be accurate and to have covered all relevant issues concerning the matter as stated which I have been asked to address.

(ii) I have endeavoured to include in my report those matters of which I have knowledge or of which I have been made aware that might adversely affect the validity of my opinion.

(iii) I have indicated the sources of all information that I have used.

(iv) I have not, without forming an independent view, included or excluded anything that has been suggested to me by others (in particular my instructing lawyers).

(v) I will notify those instructing me immediately and confirm it in writing if, for any reasons, my existing report requires any correction or clarification.

(vi) I understand that:-

(a) my report, subject to any corrections before swearing as to its correctness, will form the evidence to be given under oath or affirmation;

(b) I may be cross examined on my report by a cross examiner assisted by an expert;

(c) I am likely to be subject to public adverse criticism by the panel if it concludes that I have not taken reasonable care in trying to meet the standards set out above.

(vii) I confirm that I have not entered into any arrangements where the amount of payment of my fees is in any way dependent on the outcome of the case.

I confirm that, insofar as the facts states in my report are within my own knowledge, I have made clear which they are and I believe them to be true and that the opinions I have expressed represent my true and complete professional opinion."

Signed:

DR G PHILLIPS xxxxxx

Chapter Ten

Part 35 Rules, Getting Started and the "Necessaries"

As well as being an expert in your field you need to be familiar with and conform to the Part 35 rules which direct civil litigation in England and Wales. These are:-

1) Part 35 of the civil procedure is intended to limit the use of oral expert evidence to that which is reasonably required. In addition, where possible, matters requiring expert evidence should be dealt with by only one expert. Experts and those instructing them are expected to have regard to the guidance contained in the Guidance for the Instruction of Experts in Civil Claims 2014 at www.judiciary.gov.uk. (Further guidance on experts is contained in Annex C to the Practice Direction (Pre-Action Conduct)).

<u>Expert Evidence – General Requirements</u>

2.1 Expert evidence should be the independent product of the expert uninfluenced by the pressures of litigation.

2.2 Experts should assist the court by providing objective, unbiased opinions on matters within their expertise, and should not assume the role of an advocate.

2.3 Experts should consider all material facts, including those which might detract from their opinions.

2.4 Experts should make it clear –

(a) When a question or issue falls outside their expertise; and

(b) When they are not able to reach a definite opinion, for example because they have insufficient information.

2.5 If, after producing a report, an expert's view changes on any material matter, such change of view should be communicated to all the parties without delay, and when appropriate to the court.

2.6 (1) In a soft tissue injury claim (especially whiplash) where permission is given for a fixed cost medical report, the first report must be obtained from an accredited medical expert selected via the MedCo Portal (website at: www.medco.org.uk)

(2) The cost of obtaining a further report from an expert not listed in rule 35.4(3C) (a) to (d) is not subject to rules 45.19(2A)(b) or 45.29I(2A)(b), but the use of that expert and the cost must be justified.

(3) 'Accredited medical expert', 'fixed cost medical report', 'MedCo', and 'soft tissue injury claim' have the same meaning as in paragraph 1.1(A1), (10A), (12A) and (16A), respectively, of the RTA Protocol.

Form and Content of an Expert's Report

3.1 An expert's report should be addressed to the court and not to the party from whom the expert has received instructions.

3.2 An expert's report must:

(1) Give details of the expert's qualifications;

(2) Give details of any literature or other material which has been relied on in making the report;

(3) Contain a statement setting out the substance of all facts and instructions which are material to the opinions expressed in the report or upon which those opinions are based;

(4) Make clear which of the facts stated in the report are within the expert's own knowledge;

(5) Say who carried out any examination, measurement, test or experiment which the expert has used for the report, give the qualifications of that person, and say whether or not the test or experiment has been carried out under the expert's supervision;

(6) Where there is a range of opinion on the matters dealt with in the report –

(a) Summarise the range of opinions; and

(b) Give reasons for the expert's own opinion;

(7) Contain a summary of the conclusions reached;

(8) If the expert is not able to give an opinion without qualification, state the qualification; and

(9) Contain a statement that the expert –

(a) Understands their duty to the court, and has complied with that duty; and

(b) Is aware of the requirements of Part 35, this practice direction and the Guidance for the Instruction of Experts in Civil Claims 2014.

3.3 An expert's report must be verified by a statement of truth in the following form –

I confirm that I have made clear which facts and matters referred to in this report are within my own knowledge and which are not. Those that are within my own knowledge I confirm to be true. The opinions I have expressed represent my true and complete professional opinions on the matters to which they refer.

Part 22 deals with statements of truth. Rule 32.14 sets out the consequences of verifying a document containing a false statement without an honest belief in its truth.

Information

4 Under rule 35.9 the court may direct a party with access to information, which is not reasonably available to another party to serve on that other party a document, which records the information. The document served must include sufficient details of all the facts, tests, experiments and assumptions which underlie any part of the information to enable the party on whom it is served to make, or to obtain, a proper interpretation of the information and an assessment of its significance.

Instructions

5 Cross-examination of experts on the contents of their instructions will not be allowed unless the court permits it (or unless the party who gave the instructions

consents). Before it gives permission the court must be satisfied that there are reasonable grounds to consider that the statement in the report of the substance of the instructions is inaccurate or incomplete. If the court is so satisfied, it will allow the cross-examination where it appears to be in the interests of justice.

Questions to Experts

6.1 Where a party sends a written question or questions under rule 35.6 direct to an expert, a copy of the questions must, at the same time, be sent to the other party or parties.

6.2 The party or parties instructing the expert must pay any fees charged by that expert for answering questions put under rule 35.6. This does not affect any decision of the court as to the party who is ultimately to bear the expert's fees.

Single joint expert

7 When considering whether to give permission for the parties to rely on expert evidence and whether that evidence should be from a single joint expert the court will take into account all the circumstances in particular, whether:

(a) It is proportionate to have separate experts for each party on a particular issue with reference to –

(i) The amount in dispute;

(ii) The importance to the parties; and

(iii) The complexity of the issue;

(b) The instruction of a single joint expert is likely to assist the parties and the court to resolve the issue more speedily and in a more cost-effective way than separately instructed experts;

(c) Expert evidence is to be given on the issue of liability, causation or quantum;

(d) The expert evidence falls within a substantially established area of knowledge which is unlikely to be in dispute or there is likely to be a range of expert opinion;

(e) A party has already instructed an expert on the issue in question and whether or not that was done in compliance with any practice direction or relevant pre-action protocol;

(f) Questions put in accordance with rule 35.6 are likely to remove the need for the other party to instruct an expert if one party has already instructed an expert;

(g) Questions put to a single joint expert may not conclusively deal with all issues that may require testing prior to trial;

(h) A conference may be required with the legal representatives, experts and other witnesses which may make instruction of a single joint expert impractical; and

(i) A claim to privilege makes the instruction of any expert as a single joint expert inappropriate.

Orders

8 Where an order requires an act to be done by an expert, or otherwise affects an expert, the party instructing that expert must serve a copy of the order on the expert. The claimant must serve the order on a single joint expert.

Discussions Between Experts

9.1 Unless directed by the court, discussions between experts are not mandatory. Parties must consider, with their experts, at an early stage, whether there is likely to be any useful purpose in holding an experts' discussion and if so, when.

9.2 The purpose of discussions between experts is not for experts to settle cases but to agree and narrow issues and in particular to identify:

(i) The extent of the agreement between them;

(ii) The points of and short reasons for any disagreement;

(iii) Action, if any, which may be taken to resolve any outstanding points of disagreement; and

(iv) Any further material issues not raised and the extent to which these issues are agreed.

9.3 Where the experts are to meet, the parties must discuss and if possible agree whether an agenda is necessary, and if so attempt to agree one that helps the experts to focus on the issues which need to be discussed. The agenda must not be in the form of leading questions or hostile in tone.

9.4 Unless ordered by the court, or agreed by all parties, and the experts, neither the parties nor their legal representatives may attend experts' discussions.

9.5 If the legal representatives do attend –

(i) They should not normally intervene in the discussion, except to answer questions put to them by the experts or to advise on the law; and

(ii) The experts may if they so wish hold part of their discussions in the absence of the legal representatives.

9.6 A statement must be prepared by the experts dealing with the matters in paragraphs 9.2

9.7 Individual copies of the statements must be signed by the experts at the conclusion of the discussion, or as soon thereafter as practicable, and in any event within 7 days. Copies of the statements must be provided to the parties no later than 14 days after signing.

9.8 Experts must give their own opinions to assist the court and do not require the authority of the parties to sign a joint statement.

9.9 If an expert significantly alters an opinion, the joint statement must include a note or addendum by that expert explaining the change of opinion.

Assessors

10.1 An assessor may be appointed to assist the court under rule 35.15. Not less than 21 days before making any such appointment, the court will notify each party in writing of the name of the proposed assessor, of the matter in respect of which the assistance of the assessor will be sought and of the qualifications of the assessor to give that assistance.

10.2 Where any person has been proposed for appointment as an assessor, any party may object to that person either personally or in respect of that person's qualification.

10.3 Any such objection must be made in writing and filed with the court within 7 days of receipt of the notification referred to in paragraph 10.1 and will be taken into account by the court in deciding whether or not to make the appointment.

10.4 Copies of any report prepared by the assessor will be sent to each of the parties but the assessor will not give oral evidence or be open to cross-examination or questioning.

Concurrent expert evidence

11.1 At any stage in the proceedings the court may direct that some or all of the experts from like disciplines shall give their evidence concurrently. The following procedure shall then apply.

11.2 The court may direct that the parties agree an agenda for the taking of concurrent evidence, based upon the areas of disagreement identified in the experts' joint statements made pursuant to rule 35.12.

11.3 At the appropriate time the relevant experts will each take the oath or affirm. Unless the court orders otherwise, the experts will then address the items on the agenda in the manner set out in paragraph 11.4.

11.4 In relation to each issue on the agenda, and subject to the judge's discretion to modify the procedure

(1) The judge may initiate the discussion by asking the experts, in turn, for their views. Once an expert has expressed a view the judge may ask questions about it. At one or more appropriate stages when questioning a particular expert, the judge may invite the other expert to comment or to ask that expert's own questions of the first expert;

(2) After the process set out in (1) has been completed for all the experts, the parties' representatives

may ask questions of them. While such questioning may be designed to test the correctness of an expert's view, or seek clarification of it, it should not cover ground which has been fully explored already. In general a full cross-examination or re-examination is neither necessary nor appropriate; and

(3) After the process set out in (2) has been completed, the judge may summarise the experts' different positions on the issue and ask them to confirm or correct that summary.

Preparing Reports following Joint Instruction

Trusted experts with a good track record are occasionally asked by both solicitors involved in a case to prepare a single report to clarify the medical issues for both sides. So-called joint instruction.

Expert Meetings and Joint Reports

Normally both sides have obtained separate reports from their own experts. Frequently, after having written such reports, experts are instructed to "meet" (normally by way of a phone conference) and prepare a joint report

There are some unwritten traditions on preparing joint reports as follows:-

1) The lawyers from both sides ought to provide an agreed agenda of questions-Stick to it and don't stray into unasked territory. Sometimes only one expert has dealt with an issue on the agenda such as care needs going forward. The other may not wish to comment especially if he has not seen and examined the claimant

2) The purpose of the joint report is to set out the areas of agreement and disagreement (often with a brief resume of the reasons for the opinion of each) to allow the Court to focus on the key issues

3) Traditionally (but not set in stone) the claimant's expert is the one who does the organising of the phone conference, is the scribe and prepares the draft joint report which is then batted back and forth by e-mail (so each can fine tune their position) until a final agreed version is reached. Neither expert needs to change their position unless they feel their opinion has genuinely changed. Experts frequently agree to disagree. Always be very polite and respectful even if you think the other expert is a complete Prat!

4) On issues of different but genuinely held opinions on life expectancy NEVER split the difference (a lot of money might be at stake). That's the job of the Judge. It is preferable to agree that each expert's opinion is within an acceptable range given the inexactitude of such predictions. The Judge or Lawyers will then split the difference!

5) As to the practicalities- The claimant's expert ought to make preliminary contact (e-mail or phone) with the other Expert, establish that there is a specific agenda and agree a definite time for the conference and who will be phoning whom and who will be the scribe. It helps if the scribe sets up the draft model beforehand. Sometimes where it is clear from the reports that there are many areas of agreement, the draft can be partially written and e-mailed to the other even before the conference. Phone on the dot/ be ready and waiting for the call. Allow at least an hour for the actual conference. Prepare thoroughly beforehand. On the day double check who is to be the scribe but both ought to make notes. The

scribe draws up the Draft-this ought to be done the same day. Keep it very tight and short. I include two models as examples.

Once the final report is agreed both need to sign it-How this is done varies. One way is for each to print off a copy, sign it and post or fax to the other who on receipt of the other's signed one also signs it, copies it for their own records and then sends the version with both signatures onward to their own instructing solicitor. Ideally both sets of lawyers should get it the same day. The better way is for each to attach an electronic signature. You can buy these which turn an editable document into a sealed pdf. A simple practical way is for each to sign a scrap of paper, scan it and then copy and paste it into the document. Then e-mail it onward, thus saving time, paper and postage.

Keep a record of all the time spent and charge at your hourly rate-The scribe will bill the most. There are two main formats.

Model (1)

IN THE COUNTY COURT AT GRANCHESTER CLAIM NO: A1234567

BETWEEN:-

S B & M W

(Executors of the Estate of Mrs V B Deceased)

Claimants

The CARELESS CARE GROUP LTD

Defendant

JOINT MEDICAL REPORT BY EXPERT GERIATRICIANS

Dr X instructed by the Claimant.

Dr Y, instructed by the Defendant:

<u>To The Courts at the Request of Instructing Solicitors</u>

Further to our earlier reports in this matter, we were provided with an agenda and a telephone conference was held on the 6th July 2015. We discussed our areas of agreement and disagreement and this joint statement prepared structured around the 4 questions posed.

QUESTIONS:

VB's actual condition

Q1. How did VB's condition, both physically and mentally, change after her humerus was found to be fractured on XX/XX/XX?

A1. We agreed that there was a significant step-down both mentally and physically

Q2. Which of VB's subsequent problems (e.g. hospitalisation for 2 months, diarrhoea, the need for isolation nursing, a sacral pressure sore, loss of mobility, loss of independence, cognitive decline, etc.) would not have occurred but for the fractured humerus?

A2 We agreed that all of the above would not have occurred but for the fractured humerus

VB's hypothetical condition 'but for' the fracture

Q3. What was VB's cognitive state likely to have been, shortly before the fracture was found on XX/XX/XX?

(As requested we have referred to the medical records specified)

A3. We agreed that the independent contemporaneous medical records were poor as regards the degree of cognitive impairment and the extent of her confusion. However we agreed that there was cognitive impairment

Q4. How would VB's condition, treatment and care needs probably have progressed 'but for' her fractured humerus? If you disagree as to when VB would have required residential or nursing care, please explain why.

(As requested we have considered, what would VB's (i) mobility, (ii) cognitive state, (iii) need for increased care at home, (iv) need for residential care, and/or (v) need for nursing care, have been without the fractured humerus and its sequelae?)

A4. On this matter we were unable to reach full agreement. We agreed that even if she failed to return home she would have needed only residential (not nursing) care. Dr X remains of the opinion that she probably would have returned home. His reasoning is set out in his initial report and in his response to Part 35 questions. Dr Y remains of the opinion, that absent the arm fracture she would not have returned home and would have entered Residential Care in any event. His reasoning is set out in the opinion section of his initial report.

There were no other areas of disagreement.

Our individual expert declarations are included.

Yours faithfully

Model (2)

Dr X FRCP

Consultant Physician

Elsewhere General Hospital

Tel: xxxxxx

Email: xxxx@nhs.net

Dr Y FRCP

Consultant Geriatrician

Any other NHS Trust

Tel: xxxxxxx

Email: xxxxxx

Our Ref: X/Y/ Claimant

Your Ref: YXYXYX

11 November XX

Joint Medical Report In The Matter Of:

Claimant

RE:

Care needs/Life expectancy

To The Courts At The Request Of Instructing Solicitors

Further to our earlier reports in this matter, we were provided with an agenda and a telephone conference was held on the XX/XX/XX. We discussed our areas of agreement and disagreement and this joint statement prepared.

1) We agreed that absent his mesothelioma her late husband would have survived 15.7 years and further agreed that he could have met her needs unaided for 11 of those years. We also agreed that with help for the heavier chores and a care package for her if her needs increased he could have provided care for a further 2-3 years.

2) We were unable to fully agree upon her likely life expectancy as such estimates are always inexact. We agreed that our individual estimates were within an acceptable range. Thus she ought to survive at least 12.3 years and could have outlived her husband by surviving up to 17 years

3) Consolidating points 1 and 2, we agreed that there was only a period of up to 12 months of care provision (by her husband had he survived) which was at issue.

4) We noted her longstanding care needs but were unable to agree upon the cause owing to the paucity of recent medical records. We have set out our opinions in our reports. Dr X is of the opinion that she has a learned somatisation disorder which could improve with therapy and reduce her care needs. Dr Y's position is that whilst he cannot rule this out as a diagnosis he considers that after so many years of dependency she is very unlikely to improve and is

more likely to deteriorate due to the on-going vicissitudes of ageing.

5) There were no other areas of disagreement.

6) Our individual expert declarations are included.

Yours faithfully Yours faithfully

Getting Started

A medico-legal career can be likened to the journey of a large container ship. It starts slowly before reaching momentum and cannot be stopped quickly. New instructions come slowly at first but will grow gradually if your reputation establishes itself and increasing numbers of lawyers see your reports as they are disclosed. There are directories of "Expert Witnesses" which for a fee will include your details by way of advertising. The more reputable ones require references from solicitors. Large firms often have their own database of approved experts. If you gain a reputation for prompt quality independent reports, confidence in giving oral evidence and responding well to queries (often from the other side's solicitors) and providing succinct joint reports with the other side's expert following phone conferences, new instructions will increase. When the time comes to wind down and cease to take new instructions you will still be committed to older cases. This "run off" work will diminish with time but the odd case can still require your input for a year or more – retirement needs to be planned well ahead.

Things to consider at the outset are:-

- Your base and contact details. Hospital, home or "serviced consulting rooms" for your letterhead, reports and directory entries. These are very important as they are difficult and expensive to change in a timely manner, especially the details in directories. Solicitors will often use contact details from older reports and frequent changes will result in loss of business.

- Secretarial and other support. An accountant is advisable, a reliable secretary who knows the ropes is very useful. Some NHS secretaries will do reports in their own time but need to be your formal albeit part-time employees. If you have a digital Dictaphone you can e-mail the audio and the secretary can then type it up and e-mail back the typed up report.

- You are running a business. Do you run it as a sole trader or a limited company? Turnover greater than £80k/year will necessitate VAT registration. The accountant will advise.

- You will need MPS/MDU cover- but this + GMC, BMA, RCP etc. are tax-deductible from business profits.

- Are you prepared to take on legal aid work?

- What hourly rate will you be charging? – within reason the more you charge/hour the more highly you are thought of. A cheap hourly rate will put people off – no-one wants to commission a cheap report!

- What percentage of work, if any, are you prepared to take on "deferred terms" basis (normally your fees are paid the sooner of 2 years or end of case)? The problem is that you will have had to pay the tax on profit from fees billed (even if not paid) in the January following the end of the preceding tax year.

- Will you take instruction via agencies? To circumvent delayed payment, some solicitors instruct experts through “agencies”. For a premium charged to the solicitor, agencies will prepare the papers, screen the report and pay experts, normally within 90 days. Most agencies are reputable and efficient, often keeping a list (panel) of approved experts from a wide range of disciplines. There are however some disreputable disorganised and short-lived agencies. If agencies “go bust” experts have no redress for outstanding fees.

<u>The Necessaries</u>

Having decided all this you are in a position to create the “Necessaries” which are:-

- A professional system of invoicing, giving bank details for BACS payments – specimen invoices for both sole traders and limited companies are available to download free from the internet or copy the format which your accountant uses. {Always start invoice numbering with a random 5 figure invoice number (never 00001 as that will look as though you are a total novice) and then number them from that point consecutively}
- A medico-legal CV with terms and conditions
- A standard e-mailable response to enquiries
- A third party e-mailable response to enquiries for your PA to use for you when on holiday
- A constantly updated NON-AVAILABILITY for 12 months ready to e-mail
- A formal quote model
- A model for civilian reports with expert declaration

• A model MG11 witness statement form for police/coroner reports with their specific expert declaration and the "back sheet" which provides your contact details separate from the body of the report.

Dr J Soap FRCP chose to incorporate and practise as an independent consultant geriatrician using his home as his base and the registered address of his company, Dr J Soap & Associates Ltd. He was VAT registered and employed a part-time secretary/PA who could access their shared e-mail address which was exclusively used just for the business. He had a digital Dictaphone and could e-mail lengthy dictations for typing. Both he and his PA backed up reports on their computers and separate external hard drives to protect against them being lost. As he wrote reports on different subjects he kept an index of those subjects to use as model reports in case of future and similar requests. (His expertise was confined to a limited repertoire of areas). He created the following necessaries:-

Letterhead- for reports, correspondence and invoices etc.:

DR J SOAP – FRCP

Consultant Geriatrician

DR J SOAP & ASSOCIATES LIMITED

Geriatric Medicine Consultancy

10, Any Street

Any Town

Post Code

Tel: xxxxxxxxx

Email: xxxxxxxxx

Dr J Soap & Associates Ltd is a Limited Company • Registered in England and Wales (registered number XXXXX) Specialising in providing medico-legal reports upon the elderly.

Registered office address: 10, Any Street, Any town • VAT Registration No: 123 xxxx xxx

---

Standard responses to enquiries (Personal & Third Party)

Personal

Dear XXX,

Thank you for your enquiry of XX/XX/15. I confirm my willingness to accept instruction to prepare a report and that I foresee no conflict of interest. I normally complete such reports within a month of receipt of full instruction and accompanying papers. Cost is dependent on time which is dependent upon the volume and complexity of the material to be reviewed. Typically a single lever-arch file of average complexity takes some 5 hours to translate into a court ready report.

My terms and conditions for accepting instruction for and on behalf of Dr J Soap & Associates Ltd are as below:

Terms & Conditions:

I normally complete my reports within one month of receiving formal instruction and the relevant papers. Ideally I would prefer material scanned to a disc but paperwork is perfectly acceptable. If papers are sent please specify if you need them returning. If not so specified, my default position is to retain papers for a month in the event of queries, then archive off site temporarily pending shredding. Shredding is done by a commercial company roughly every four months.

My current standard rate is charged at £XXX per hour + VAT, on the basis of settlement within 60 days.

It makes no commercial sense for this small company to accept significant numbers of instructions on a "deferred terms basis." However I appreciate that interim payment of such disbursements before the end of the case can also be problematic for smaller firms. I am therefore prepared to agree in advance to deferred payment (for up to two years or end of case – whichever is sooner) at an enhanced rate of £XXX.00 per hour + VAT. I limit this to a maximum of 12 such cases per financial year which I allocate on the basis of first come first served. I have now filled my quota for this financial year.

I do not take instruction at legal aid rates. I am now declining instructions to prepare screening reports at a fixed fee, where the fee is unlikely to reflect the time needed to produce the sort of quality report which you have a right to expect. To deal properly with these, less than 3 hours is unrealistic.

My fees for attending Court are £XXXX per day + VAT and expenses. I apply a cancellation fee of 50% if the dates are cancelled within two weeks, and full rate if cancellation is less than two days.

Formal instruction will be taken as acceptance of these terms and conditions. Upon request I can advise whether I can still offer deferred terms this year or if I can no longer offer deferred terms this year. I attach my

CV giving further information and look forward to hearing from you.

With kind regards,

Jo Soap

Third Party Response

Dear XXXX,

Thank you for your enquiry. Dr Soap is currently on leave until 7th of November and upon his return he is potentially in court for up to a week. He is however likely to confirm his willingness to accept instruction to prepare a report and will advise as to whether there is any conflict of interest. He normally completes such reports within a month of receipt of full instruction and accompanying papers. However new reports are unlikely to be started before mid-November. Cost is dependent on time which is dependent upon the volume and complexity of the material to be reviewed. Typically a single lever-arch file of average complexity takes some 5 hours to translate into a court ready report. Any home visits for assessment will add to the cost. Meanwhile I attach his CV giving further information including his "Terms and Conditions" and full contact details. I am sure he will respond himself once he is back.

With kind regards,

Emma Royd

For and on behalf of Dr J Soap

Invoice Model – Examples can be downloaded from the internet to which company details and VAT registration can be added as per the letterhead.

Non-Availability Model

To whom it may concern,

At present my NON-AVAILABILITY from 1st October 2015 for 12 months is as follows:-

i) 16/12/15 (Conference with counsel)

ii) 22/12/15 to 16/01/16 (In Australia)

iii) 21/01/16 to 28/02/16 (Two Crown Court trials-my dates yet to be specified)

iv) 18/04/16 to 26/04/16 (Crown Court trial-my dates yet to be specified)

v) 11/05/16 to 13/05/16 (Inquest)

This could, of course, change and I have to work on the basis of "first come first served" so the sooner you pin me down the better all round.

Jo Soap

Formal Quote Model

Our Ref: New Instruction – Alleged Assault on Jane Doe

URN 20XXXXXXX15

8th June 2015

To Oxford Police

1) I am Dr Joseph Soap and I hold the qualifications MBBCh (Bachelor of Medicine and Bachelor of Surgery), and have been a Fellow of the Royal College of Physicians of London since 1993. I held the position of full time consultant geriatrician within the XXXX Teaching Hospitals between 1982 and 2011. I was also an Honorary Lecturer in the University Department of Medicine. Following re-organisation within my main

hospital base I took the opportunity to retire from the NHS, in good standing, and In May 2011 entered full time independent practice.

2) My daily practice involved dealing with the full range of medical illness, which affects the elderly. This included the assessment of injuries often in association with confusion and dementing illness.

3) I have been asked by Oxford Police to provide a formal quote for preparation of a report to assist with the investigation of the injuries sustained. I have been provided with the details on MG3, statements, photographs and hospital notes in a well-organised bundle of material approximating to just over 100 sheets.

4) I confirm my willingness to accept instruction to prepare a full and detailed report of evidential quality and that I have no conflict of interest. I routinely complete such reports within a month of receipt of full instruction and accompanying papers and will complete this report speedily. Cost is dependent on time which is dependent upon the volume and complexity of the material to be reviewed. I am no longer taking instructions for work at legal aid rates. I charge at my current standard rate of £XXXper hour + VAT, on the basis of settlement within 60 days. I estimate the time that I shall spend on the matter to produce such a report will be no more than 3 hours.

5) My quote is therefore for up to £XXX.00 + VAT for a full report on an MG11 form which I shall complete within days of my quote being deemed acceptable.

Yours sincerely

DR J Soap FRCP

Consultant Physician in Geriatric Medicine

MG11 Witness Statement Model

Top tips:

1) The police will e-mail you a blank form on request which has the “back sheet” for your contact details

2) The URN is the “Unique reference Number” normally issued after charging

3) Do NOT get your signature witnessed (that is only necessary if you are under 18 years old)

4) The first page needs signing at the top and bottom, all others at the bottom only

5) The last paragraph should be the expert declaration as below:

“I confirm that I understand that my overriding duty as an expert is to provide independent assistance to the court by way of objective unbiased opinion within my sphere of expertise both in preparing reports and in giving oral evidence. I have complied and will continue to comply with that duty.”

6) Only sign it off once you are sure that you have seen everything you need and the senior investigating officer (SIO) is happy that you have covered all the areas required. This reduces the danger of producing serial mini reports with the potential for contradictory opinions as the evidence unfolds.

THE MG11

WITNESS STATEMENT

CJ Act 1967, s.9; MC Act 1980, ss.5A(3) (a) and 5B; Criminal Procedure Rules 2005 , Rule 27.1

URN

Statement of: Dr Joseph Soap

Age if under 18: Over 18 (if over 18 insert 'over 18') Occupation: Consultant Physician

This statement (consisting of X page(s) each signed by me) is true to the best of my knowledge and belief and I make it knowing that, if it is tendered in evidence, I shall be liable to prosecution if I have wilfully stated in it anything which I know to be false, or do not believe to be true.

Signature: Date: 29/05/13

Tick if witness evidence is visually recorded ☐ *(supply witness details on rear)*

1) Further to my earlier report/statement of XXXX I have been asked to ......